Flight Attendant Joe

Joe Thomas

Joe Thomas writes a blog called Flight Attendant Joe
www.flightattendantjoe.com

Also by Joe Thomas

Fasten Your Seat Belts
And Eat Your Fucking Nuts

I dedicate this book to every flight attendant on planet Earth. If you are currently reading this book in 2274, Mars too!

In memory of Alison Strickland.

Table of Contents

Foreword
By Laura Jean Salerno

Asking an actor to write the foreword for your new book sounds a bit risky to me. Why? Well let's face it, at the end of the day actors are known for being a bit self-involved. This could easily turn into a story all about me, so before we go down that rabbit hole let's talk about the man of the hour. I can confidently say that Joe is a good man. And I've had plenty of experience with douche bag guys; I live in Los Angeles, which is basically a dumpster fire of human garbage.

Not everyone. Relax!

But more often than not I would bet on douche bag.

I think we're getting off topic. Let's circle back.

JOE! I liked Joe right away. Instantly. Some people you just meet and there are sparks and electricity. It was both weird and wonderful because I didn't feel those sparks in my lady garden which is usually my signal to evacuate a relationship (Get it? Flight attendant humor). Nope. I felt it in my soul, my heart, and my abs. Joe had me doubled over as if I had just finished my first CrossFit class. I was sore, but it was the right kind of sore. I hadn't laughed that much in ages. It was a real tennis match of wit and humor for three days straight, and Joe was the ultimate partner. He would "yes, and" each set up and knock every joke right out of the aircraft. I actually couldn't wait to wake up and go to work knowing that no matter what ridiculous situation we had to deal with for the day Joe would make me laugh. It was contagious. The crew, the passengers, and everyone we interacted with all thought we had known each other for years. Daily disasters became small hiccups when coupled with a roaring belly laugh heard in adjacent terminals. And what was even more intoxicating was getting him to bust out laughing at something I had said.

Joe was fascinated I worked in TV/Film and had "famous" friends. He was shocked that I could have an episode of a well-known show currently airing and still be serving people Diet Cokes on the weekend. Hell, so was I. I certainly thought I would be picking up more dudes numbers on the plane than I would be picking up dirty diapers.

I'll admit I will do almost anything in the name of humor and I have no problem with cracking a joke at my own expense if the reward is hearing someone roaring with laughter. Given the option of getting laughs or getting laid, I'm going for laughs because I'm probably going to be faking it the first few times anyway. True, organic laughter is one thing I never have to pretend, which brings me back to Joe and his new book *Flight Attendant Joe*.

I was so excited to get my hands on Joe's new book and see him pull back the galley curtain yet again. Not only do you get the inside scoop on flight attendant life, flight cancellations, and the struggles of delays, you also get it from the perspective of a seasoned professional. A seasoned professional who has learned how to juggle people, friendships, personalities, with wit, humor, and compassion. How life struggles don't just disappear at work and how close quarters, late van rides, and unactivated hotel key cards at three in the morning magnify the stress of the industry and a fourteen hour duty day.

This book is a juicy read. It's real and stripped down. It's honest and still full of Joe's signature humor and dirty jokes.

If you've purchased this book, you clearly have a sense of humor, good taste, and are most likely in the airline industry or know someone who is. Maybe you are a frequent flyer with an inappropriate taste for comedy. Whatever the reason, thank you for supporting my friend and helping him build his 401K so he may one day retire and not end up in the *Guinness World Records* as the oldest living flight attendant. I look forward to the day I'm spoon feeding him in his nursing home as he loudly tells me inappropriate dick jokes because let's face it, some things will never change.

I would say the moral of this intro and the set up for the book you are about to read is; not all flight attendants are assholes. We are all in that magical metal tube together praying we get from point A to point B in the most routine way possible. We have good days and bad days.

Get ready; this book will take you on a fascinating and hilarious trip from wheels up to wheels down. Oh, and most importantly, we always appreciate it when you bring us a box of chocolates. Forrest Gump said it best; you never know what you're going to get and that has never been truer than on an airplane.

Fly safe birdies. Enjoy the ride.

Prepare For Departure

Dear Reader,

Welcome.

Greetings, salutations, and a few translations:

To the Latin Americans: Bienvenido

To the Lesbians: Home Depot

To the Russians: Dobro Pozhalovat'

To the Homosexual men: Heeeeeeeeeey

To the Portuguese: Bem Vinda.

To the Transgender Community: Don't Even Go There, Joe!

To the Chinese: Huānyíng

To the Trump Supporters: White Power

Let me go ahead and stop right there.

I am elated you purchased a copy of this book. I'm thrilled it's finally completed and in your hands ready to be consumed. Again, thank you from the bottom of my flat feet. Yes, I have flat feet. They are terrible for hiking long distances in the mountains, but fantastic when being drafted into the military. To be honest, I don't even know if having flat feet keeps you out of the military. All I know is my mother drilled it into my head that I would never get drafted because of this deformity.

I have flat feet. And I haven't been drafted — you do the math.

I've said it before, and I'll repeat it, I never thought I'd write a book. Never in my wildest pornographic dreams did I think this would come to fruition. But here I am, not only have I written one book, I've written two. Two books? Who do I think I am? Stephen King?

Not even close.

Although now that I've brought up Stephen King, I think I'll share a short story.

The year was 2001, and I was spending a sunny afternoon shopping at my favorite bookstore in Sarasota, Florida. While perusing the books, I happened upon Stephen King thumbing through a book. Yes, you read that correctly, Stephen King. The author of *Carrie. Christine. Stand By Me. Misery.* That Stephen King. I'd name all his work, but then this book would be the size of *It*.

See what I did there?

Now don't ask me what book he was flipping through, or what section of the bookstore we were standing in — I will never remember — and anyway, I'm talking about Stephen King… I was in complete fucking shock.

As I walked up and down the aisle, pretending to search for a book, I stumbled upon an employee of the bookstore and whispered, "Is that Stephen King?"

She giggled, "Oh yes. Mr. King comes in whenever he's in town."

"He lives here?" I couldn't believe it.

"He owns a home here. We just let him be. I think he enjoys not being bothered."

She lost me at, "… owns a home here."

I had a new agenda, and it had nothing to do with buying books. It had to do with becoming Stephen King's best friend. After it took him awhile to pick out a few books — he takes his time when it comes to reading material — he purchased the books and walked out of the store. I followed him outside but quickly lost him.

After craning my neck around the parking lot for a few minutes, I concluded that he was long gone. I was sad but extremely excited. I called a friend and yelled into my flip phone as I walked towards my car. "You won't believe this. I just bumped into Stephen King and…"

Before I finished my sentence, I stopped when a small convertible roadster backed out of a parking spot and blocked me from continuing. As I spoke the words S-T-E-P-H-E-N K-I-N-G into the phone, I realized he was behind the wheel of the roadster.

With the convertible top down, we made eye contact in his rearview mirror. I forgot about the phone call, pointed at him, and screamed, "STEPHEN."

He sped off without looking back.

Stephen, if you are reading this, I'm still holding out hope that one day we'll pick up where our friendship left off.

This story has thrown me way off track. Where exactly was I?

Now I remember. But before I continue, I might as well share a confession. When I sat down to pen this introduction, I had no idea what I was going to write. No clue. That's not a lie. No Pinocchio nose growth here. The Stephen King memory unfolded as I typed on the laptop. That's why I love to write. I might not know what I want to say — or how I want to say it — but the journey to the final product is always an exciting ride.

The underlying theme of this book is ego. My ego. Your ego. Everyone's ego. I'm obsessed with ego, and when I started putting this book together, the stories I decided to tell all seemed to revolve around managing egos.

Everything orbits around egos.

We spend our lives dodging people's egos; at our jobs, in our homes, or picking up dinner at the grocery store. On the airplane, where every passenger believes they have boarded their private jet. Ego runs rampant wherever we go. Most people deny their egos, but I embrace my ego. I have an ego boner, and that's how it often feels, like a raging boner that rarely goes flaccid.

And you will soon experience my ego boner first hand. Along with enough dick jokes, blasphemy, and inappropriate humor to last you a few years.

Side note: That was your disclaimer!

Side note two: I'm glad my mother is dead, she'd never have been able to handle reading about my ego boner.

This book is part of my journey. It's the point where Flight Attendant Joe and Joe Thomas converge. Over the past ten years as a flight attendant, I've heard, "You're just a flight attendant," on more than one occasion. But flight attendants are not just flight attendants; we are much more. We have lives. We have loved. We've lost, and we've won. We are not only servers in the sky; we are leaders of our destiny.

Wow. That was some sappy shit.

These are my stories, and they are incredibly personal. When I sat down to write these essays, I wanted them to come from my true feelings at the time they occurred. You may sense that I am perplexed at times, sad at times, and fucking furious all the other times. But keep in mind, as we all know, time heals our scars.

Or at least most of them.

Time has healed my wounds towards people I have felt wronged me during certain times in my life. I think that's all we can ask for, the ability to let go of the rage and move on with our lives.

I have done my best to share them as truthful as possible. Some people may dispute certain situations, conversations, and outcomes, but what I reveal in this book has been plucked directly from my memory and the data I've kept from journals throughout the years.

For protection and safety, I've changed names, dates, years, cities, airline bases, and other identifying information to assure anonymity.

With that out of the way, I encourage you to grab a blanket, an adult beverage, a copy of this book — your genitals if you must — and join me as I maneuver through a world of extreme personalities and excessive selfdom... including my own.

And plenty of crude jokes.

Sincerely,

Flight Attendant Joe

I Wrote A Book:
July 13, 2016

"Where are you?" my manager, Garon, asked me over the phone while my head spun around trying to pull my thoughts together.

"What? Where am I?" I sputtered out moving my cell phone from ear to ear trying to hear him.

"Yes. I want to know exactly where you were the moment the book published."

I looked around the JFK flight attendant lounge. It was jam-packed with flight attendants seated in overstuffed chairs, and it felt like the heat was turned up to 1000 degrees, "I'm in JFK. My flight is delayed. I'm sweating my fucking ass off, and I'm exhausted."

He laughed. I didn't. I find whenever I tell someone who thinks the flight attendant life is fabulous — that it, in fact, is not all pilot blowjobs and free flights — they tend to laugh at my shitty day. It's not that people are mean about it, they just don't want the fantasy of what they think a flight attendant does to go away.

I can't blame them. Sadly for me, that fantasy was ruined on day two of the job. Alright, I am exaggerating — day four.

There was no time to relish in the fact that I had just published my first book. Seconds before my call with Garon, *Fasten Your Seat Belts And Eat Your Fucking Nuts* uploaded for ebook sales. I had no opportunity to celebrate. I had no time to be excited. At that moment, I was playing the role of a flight attendant (not a newly published author), so before I could step back and throw myself a fiesta, I had to finish the day serving demanding airline passengers.

I expected that to be difficult, and my expectations did not fail me. If there is one thing working in the airline industry does, it's keeping you grounded and your ego in check. The moment you feel a few inches off the ground from euphoria the airline will swiftly slap you on the top of the head like a Pez dispenser to bring you back down to Earth.

It was July 13, and I was one flight away from ending a four-day trip. Sadly, I had no time to be excited about the success of finally publishing my book, a project that had taken me 34 months to complete.

When I hung up the phone with Garon, I put my luggage beside a big black leather chair and flopped myself into it. I pulled off my clip-on tie from the top button of my shirt, undid that top button, and sighed so deep I woke up the flight attendant sitting next to me.

"I did it," I said out loud, but just to myself. I wanted to hear the words come to life — to make it real. For so long, it felt as if I was merely typing away on my laptop doing my best impression of Jack Torrance from *The Shining*. Now it was over. All the hours of writing, editing, screaming, drinking wine, and procrastinating had paid off.

I smiled for a brief second, and then the lead flight attendant walked over to me, "The plane just landed. We gotta get to the gate."

Celebrating the publication of a book should last longer than a two-second smile, but there was no celebrating for me in my near future. At least not for the next few hours.

I buttoned up my shirt again, latched on my tie in a fuck-you sort of way and followed Melanie through the crew lounge and into the airport.

It had been a fantastic four-day trip. Melanie had been with the airline for a little under a year, and she was incredible. One of the best new flight attendants I had ever worked with — if you consider being a flight attendant for a year 'new'. I do. Anything under a year is new. I also call 25-year-old adults kids. I thank being in my 40's for that.

Melanie and I walked up to the gate and introduced ourselves to Captain Mike. A short, oversized beefy Italian guy who was married, but hard to believe could be anyone's type. I take that back — he was more like the 2 a.m. type. The guy you wouldn't think twice about at 9:00 p.m. while out having drinks with friends, but then might consider at 2:00 a.m. when the lights came on. I figured he was handsome as a young man, but all the UV rays from working inside the flight deck for 20 years had finally caught up with him.

Captain Mike was all smiles, "Alright kids, we got a 45-minute flight to Boston and no mechanicals that I can see on the release paperwork. We're not armed. Don't worry about checking on us because it's such a short flight."

I wasn't planning on it, but I just stood there smiling.

He continued, "What do you guys do after we get to Boston?"

Melanie answered, "We're scheduled to deadhead back to Cleveland."

I jumped in, "I'm going directly home to California."

Captain Mike looked at me, "What time is your commute?"

"We have time. There's about two hours between flights."

He smiled, grabbed his luggage, and started down the jet bridge, "Good. I don't want you to miss your flight home."

Once the cleaners were off the airplane, we did a quick — but thorough — check of our emergency equipment and began boarding. About 20 minutes into boarding a long-haired brunette woman with glasses made her way to the back of the airplane. I watched as she marched herself down the narrow aisle staring directly into my eyes. The way she marched left me feeling uneasy, but she didn't have her hand extended straight out in front of her, so I relaxed a bit. It's difficult enough dealing with asshole airline passengers, add being a Nazi to that, and I might as well just call in fatigue.

I also didn't break eye contact. This scenario plays out all the time, and I treat it as if I've come face-to-face with a mountain lion on a hiking trail. I haven't, but if I ever did, this is how I would respond: never break eye contact. The first to break eye contact is the weaker one, and on my airplane, I'm the mountain lion.

Standing next to the lavatory, with my arms folded defensively, I surveyed her as she continued towards me. She abruptly stopped a few rows from where I was standing and let go of her suitcase handle. Her gaze broke from mine (I won that fight) and her eyes darted around looking for any available overhead bin space. There was none.

You might ask me, "Joe, why weren't you proactive and immediately run to the passenger to assist her with her bag?"

The answer is simple: I didn't like the way she was staring at me. That, and I wanted to see how this baggage dilemma played out. There are two ways a situation like this will usually go. The first, the passenger asks in a non-aggressive manner about where to store their bag. The second — which is way more popular among airline passengers — is the demanding holier-than-thou delivery.

She looked up to the left. Then the right. Again to the left. Then straight back to me. I stood there smiling. I believe it was my devilish smile that set her off. She threw her arms up in the air, hitting the handle of her suitcase which caused it to fling backward towards the passenger directly behind her, "What am I supposed to do with my bag?"

I pointed a few rows away, "Ma'am if you go back a few rows, there's some empty bin space."

"But that's not where I'm sitting. I want my bag where I'm sitting."

"The bins are full; there's no room. Why did you wait so long to board?"

Entirely the wrong thing to say, but it felt great. The passenger didn't feel the same way I did. "What does it matter when I board? There should be a space for my bag."

Where did she go to airline passenger school? Because I have been to airline passenger school — aka flight attendant training — and never has that been written in any policy.

But I kept my cool, "If you don't want to place your bag a few rows up from your seat, we can check it."

"What kind of option is that?" She stood there as if I was kicking her and her bag off the airplane. It hadn't come to that yet, but I wasn't ruling it out. To be honest, I was shocked her cell phone hadn't made an appearance documenting the entire conversation.

With a softer tone, I repeated her options, "You can place the bag in the overhead bin a few rows ahead, or we can check it for you at no cost."

She stood there for a few moments, holding up a dozen other passengers behind her, and projected the dirtiest look towards me that I had ever received on an airplane. And I get dirty looks on every flight. It's guaranteed. I can count on dirty looks like I can count on runway construction at JFK.

But this look was different. It triggered me in a wrong way. Instantly, and without having the control to stop myself, I spit out, "Don't look at me like that." It was such a shock that as the words tumbled out of my mouth, I mentally started looking for another job.

My tone not only startled me but must have frightened the shit out of her because without saying another word, she retraced her steps a few rows and quickly placed her bag in an available space in the overhead bin and took her seat.

There were no further words regarding our interaction. During service, when I handed this lady her drink, I wanted to lean in and quietly ask, "Now was that bag situation so fucking hard?" But I found a shred of control and decided to leave well enough alone.

Soon after, the rest of the passengers were boarded, in their seats, and we were all ready for departure. Let me rephrase that, everyone was prepared for departure except for the airplane.

After the safety demonstration and final compliance check, I found myself standing in the back galley — 15 minutes after our scheduled departure — and noticed we had yet to pull away from the gate. That's when the questions and call bells started ringing. After answering a few questions from passengers in the last few rows, I picked up the interphone and called Captain Mike inside the flight deck.

"This is Mike."

"Hey Mike, it's Joe. What's going on?"

He paused. That's never a great sign, it's not even a good sign, "Joe, seems we have a little problem," then another pause, "but you should still catch your flight home."

Melanie was on the other end of the interphone, but let me do all the talking. Possibly exhausted from our three previous flights, words had escaped her. Thankfully, they hadn't avoided me. "What do you mean? What's the problem?"

Mike giggled, "We're too heavy. They miscalculated loading our fuel. They gave us too much. We can take off, but we will be too heavy to land."

I looked down the aisle studying the backs of the passenger's heads for a second and then crouched down next to the back airplane door, so the passenger's in the last row wouldn't hear me, "Too much fuel? On a 30 minute flight? That makes no sense. Just take it out."

"It's not that easy. Maintenance is looking into what we can do. We may have to remove some luggage, or — if it comes to it — take some passengers off and put them on the next flight."

At that moment, I didn't give a fuck if they threw luggage and passengers out on the tarmac and ran them over.

"Alright, Mike. This situation isn't good. I'll be highly upset if I miss my commute."

"You've got time. No worries, Big Joe. Okay, let me call tech ops. I'll let you know what's going on."

We hung up the interphones. My first instinct was to yell out a few choice words, but I held them back, and for a good reason. When I turned around, a female passenger was standing in the galley, "What's going on? Why are we delayed?"

Trying to explain this to a passenger, when I didn't fully understand it, caused my heart to start palpitating. Really, why was it so hard to get the fuel out of the airplane? Grab a straw and start sucking. We were at JFK. I know for a fact that only a few hundred feet away from where our plane was parked — in the bowels of the airport — tucked away behind a maze of hallways, was the flight attendant lounge stocked full of gay men ready to start sucking. Gay men that have been preparing for this exact type of event since high school. Or, if they were unlucky, camping with their Boy Scout Scoutmaster.

Airlines have special ops teams who sit around waiting for the day a catastrophe occurs to be deployed to save lives. It's wonderful. A hurricane takes out Miami-Dade County and — SWOOSH — these brave men and women take weeks out of their lives to travel to ground zero and assist victims. They are heroes. Sure, they probably do it so they can get out of their daily routine, but who am I to judge. I once had surgery so I could take Christmas and New Years off.

The point being, if my airline can fund a team for those types of emergencies, why not have the same for over fueled airplanes? And staff them with the homosexuals already employed. It's a genius plan. Management would barely have to put any effort into advertising.

I can imagine the note pinned to the bulletin board in the flight attendant lounge:

> Dear Male Homosexual Flight Attendants,
>
> Are you into helping others who are in need? Into excitement? A little danger? Well, (possibly a lot of risks if you swallow) look no further. We are searching for a highly qualified group of men who will be able to drop everything they are doing to help the airline in the event of a fuel emergency.
>
> All you have to do is bring your lips and a desire to please — we'll handle the rest! If you are interested and have the capability of sucking a golf ball through a straw, email the Fuel Sucking Team at wesuckitrightout@airline.com.
>
> Sincerely,
> Your Flight Attendant Management Team

Just as I was about to tell this lady to take her seat, because I had no idea what to say about the fuel, Captain Mike came over the PA to relay the same message to them as he told me moments before.

"Ladies and gentlemen, as you can tell, we have not pulled away from the gate. It seems that they loaded us with too much fuel and maintenance is here trying to figure out a game plan. We can take off with no issues, but we won't be able to land safely. Once we know more, we will let you know. Thanks for your patience. Flight attendants, please disarm your doors and prepare to reopen them."

In the airline industry, if something is going to go wrong, it's always going to be on your last flight of the day.

Confusion hung in the air like a thick mist. The murmurs and questions around the last few rows were unanimous, how the hell do we have too much fuel?

A full hour past and we were still at the gate. Passengers became increasingly agitated and feared they would miss their connecting flights. At the hour mark, Melanie and I decided to walk through the airplane offering bottled water to the irked passengers to tide them over. Have you ever tried making peace with people who are in danger of missing their connecting flights to destinations around the world by offering them a bottle of water? I am shocked we didn't walk off that airplane with cases of water shoved up our asses.

As I handed out the last bottle of water on my tray, the interphone chime rang like the buzzer on *Jeopardy.* I had a feeling I still wouldn't get the question right. I pushed past the last few rows while hands reached out grabbing at me like flesh-eating zombies. As they reached out to me — I don't know why they thought that was a good idea — each person continued yelling out the same questions over and over again.

If I had had a white poster board and black marker, it would have been easier jotting down a few select answers to their questions and placing the board at the front of the airplane. Honestly, I can't recall each inquiry. But if my memory serves me right, the answers went something like: I don't know when we are leaving. I'm sorry you're missing your connecting flight — so am I. The airline doesn't pay for hotels. Listen, why don't you all just fuck off and die.

You know, answers that matter.

I picked up the interphone, and it was Melanie, "How's it going back there?"

"It's good. The passengers are grabbing at me like extras from *The Walking Dead*."

She barely giggled, "This sucks. I'm stressing out from these people and their questions."

I took that as a good enough reason to check on her, so after handing additional bottles of water to the last few rows (I still had a job to do), I made my way through the airplane to the front to check on Melanie. She was holding herself together, but her exhaustion and frustration were colossal. I understood. My body felt the urge to collapse at row one, but the idea of missing my commute kept me energized.

"You doing okay?" I asked her as she stood in the galley staring back at me.

"I'm exhausted, and we haven't left yet. This is terrible."

To be honest, we had only been waiting for a little over an hour. It wasn't the end of the world, but I didn't want to make Melanie feel bad.

"I'm sure we will be leaving soon." I stuck my head into the flight deck, "Mike. What are you guys trying to do to us?"

He turned around and snickered, "Joe. You know what? If you were any cuter, I'd ask you for your number."

"What's my phone number have to do with a blow-job?"

"Oh, you are feisty. I like that." He let out a robust laugh. I didn't have the heart to tell him that I had been merely joking around regarding the blowjob and that the only fat Italian sausage I'd be having anytime soon would be on my pizza — or in a hoagie roll with some peppers, onions, and marinara — not attached to my captain. Especially a captain who aided in the possibility of me missing my commute flight home.

After checking on Melanie to make sure she wasn't about to go postal on the passengers in the front row, I walked down the aisle towards the back galley in record speed. The trick during a rolling delay is, never make eye contact with the passengers. Never. What's a rolling delay? That's a delayed flight, and the airline has no clue when it will depart. It's like being in delayed limbo. Will it take off in five minutes? Will it take off in five hours? Nobody has a clue. That's a rolling delay.

But let's get back to the discussion of making eye contact with the passengers, DON'T! Once you lock eyes with one of these thirsty little savages, it's all over. Even if they don't need anything, the moment you look into their eyes, they will signal you for something. A bottle of water. The time. To pass along a dirty diaper. Ask you random stupid questions that have no place being asked on an airplane. Making eye contact is a grave mistake. Ask any flight attendant. As I swiftly moved towards the back, a passenger got me. It was an accident, a rookie mistake if you will. I had been scanning the floor as I walked down the aisle and looked up too soon. The moment that happened, some crazy bitch got me.

20

"Excuse me," she raised her voice and her hand, "What's going on?"

I had no clue. Still in the dark with the rest of the passengers, I figured that type of honestly might seem like I was hiding something. And I was, I was hiding the fact that I seriously had no clue what was going on. Passengers don't like hearing short answers from the flight attendant. They want a dissertation on the ins and outs of everything happening at that exact moment. I understand, but the sad part is, we are usually just as ignorant as them in these situations. I did my best at playing it off like the true professional I am, "We should be leaving shortly."

This lady was Russian. I do not have the best luck with Russian passengers. A few years ago, on an airplane high up in the sky, I had a Russian passenger named Ivan shriek at me. Was it because I checked his bag? No. Was it because I accidentally poured hot coffee on his crotch? Nope. I had innocently skipped over him during beverage service. In my defense, he was sleeping, but because of my mistake, he spent a decent amount of the flight spraying his lousy breath stench all over me. There was no way I was putting up with that shit again. Dealing with an angry Russian, on a flight not even destined for Russia, is something you only want to experience once in your life.

As I had expected, my answer wasn't sufficient. The lady spoke loudly, "We are going to miss our connecting flight. What are you going to do for me?"

Those eight words caught me off guard, "I'm sorry, what was that? What am I going to do for you?"

"Yes. It is all your fault."

She was apparently referring to the airline; nothing at that moment was my fault. But as most flight attendants forget — I am guilty of this on many occasions — is that while we are in uniform, and on the airplane, we are the face of the airline at that moment. Everything that happens during that flight is OUR fault. It sucks, but I would argue with anyone who says they have never blamed a rank-and-file employee for their disappointment with a whole company.

I am guilty of this as well, so I will share a story that makes me look like a complete asshole. And an egotistical asshole I have been.

The drama I am about to tell took place inside a Subway restaurant. Don't judge me on my diet; you'll have plenty to criticize when this quick tale is over. I usually order healthy food from Subway, but on this specific day, I wanted something unhealthy and tasty, I walked into the restaurant, stepped up to the order line and with a smile made my request, "Hi. Can I have a footlong meatball sub, with extra pickles, provolone cheese, and barbeque sauce?"

The underpaid employee stared at me and answered me with a flat, "We're out of barbeque sauce."

It was as if she told me the meatballs would give me trichinosis.

"What? You're out of barbeque sauce. Why?"

"We only carried it for a few months. It was for a special sandwich."

Logic flew out the door, "Are you fucking kidding me? I have been thinking about this sandwich all day."

She practically shrunk in size, "I'm sorry, sir. We don't have it."

"This is ridiculous. What kind of business is this? Why don't you have barbeque sauce? You make sandwiches, right?" My irrational logic was to think that if I got angry enough, she'd run to the back of the restaurant and unearth one last bottle of barbeque sauce to make me happy. The same thing happens on the airplane when a passenger asks for something — I say that we don't have it, and they stare at me like I am going to change my position and realize I was wrong.

That never happens. It didn't occur at Subway either, "Is there anything else I can make you?"

"No. I don't want anything!" By this time, if I were a toddler in daycare, I would have been placed in my much needed time out. "I will never come back here! You have lost a customer!"

Now remember, in case you lost focus, this was all over barbeque sauce. I'll repeat it barbeque sauce. I am not proud of this moment, but it's essential to explain… barbeque sauce.. I stormed out while she stood watching me have a mental breakdown over — I know I've said it three times — BARBEQUE SAUCE.

When I hit my tenth step from the building, I realized what a horrible human being I had been to this poor girl who just wanted to make me a sandwich. I forwent any rational thinking and went straight for her jugular. I imagined her entire existence was to make my life an utter living hell. I took out the idea that she was a human being, with feelings and emotions, and directly looked at her like she was the Subway restaurant. A person, but a person who represented Subway.

I turned around and started back towards the restaurant. If the employee had attacked me with a baseball bat, I would have deserved it. I stepped inside and before she could say anything I projected out my humble apology, "I'm so very sorry. I can't believe I acted like that. I feel terrible. I know this isn't your fault. I work in customer service, and I'm ashamed of myself. I'm sorry."

She stared at me for a moment, probably trying to remember where the bat was, and without breaking a sweat responded, "That's cool. Did you want me to make you a sandwich?"

That interaction told me two things about this girl; one, she must be verbally abused enough that my words just bounced off her during my earlier rant, and second — she was a goddamn professional.

Behavior from human beings like that happens quite often on the airplane. I stand corrected, it happens everywhere, including a Subway restaurant.

My exhaustion finally settled in, and it came out in my tone towards the Russian, "Nothing is my fault. We're all stuck on this airplane together. We can arrange for you to take another flight if you'd like."

Her two teenage children were seated in the row across from her and immediately jumped in, "We're sorry about our mother, she's just worried." They looked past me and directed their gaze towards her aisle seat, "Mother stop giving him a hard time."

After waiting a few moments, and looking back and forth from the Russian to her kids and back again, I continued walking to the galley.

There was a commuting flight attendant in my galley, "I had to get out of my seat for a while. How long have we been sitting here?"

I looked at my watch, "Almost an hour and a half. Can I get you something to drink?"

"No. But thank you. I hope we don't cancel. I need to get home tonight."

Let me stop for a moment to explain the situation. I was annoyed, tired, and heated from my Russian encounter. I think I can speak on behalf of many Americans when I say; I don't have time for Russians interfering in my shit. After that, the last thing I wanted was engaging in small talk with another flight attendant. I had only checked on Melanie because I felt it was my duty as the senior flight attendant on the trip. My patience waned, any patience left would be saved for passenger encounters.

Talking to this guy was the last thing I wanted to do. Why? I may come off as bitchy, but it was his teeth. I never have, in my forty-something years on this planet, ever seen teeth that shade of yellow. I wouldn't call them yellow, more gold. Gold with dirt scattered throughout. The kind of teeth that would make a dentist scream out, "Margaret, cancel the rest of my appointments… for the week."

Was I wrong? I thought for a second, maybe I was fatigued, and my eyes were playing tricks on me. Does that happen? Is there a level of exhaustion which makes us unable to decipher the difference between plaque and gold plating? My curiosity peaked but getting close enough to find out was out of the question. I stepped away from him as far as humanly possible, but it was a small regional jet galley — I could only go so far before the only option was opening the airplane door and jumping 10 feet to my death. I contemplated it for a brief moment. Why not? I was probably missing my commute home anyway, so what did I have to lose? It's incredible what we will consider when trying to escape a fucked up mouth. Even George Washington refused to smile in front of people. He knew his teeth were jacked up, but not this flight attendant, he smiled as if he had won the lottery.

I tried everything to avoid him, but he refused to leave the galley. My next option was to keep busy, so that's what I did. I opened the lavatory door to do a security check and found that in an hour, male passengers had pissed all over the lavatory floor. I'm going out on a limb and blaming the guys on this one. If it was, in fact, women, there is no hope for the planet.

A pile of toilet paper laid crumbled on the floor. With a quick glance, it seemed a few people had taken substantial shits without a courtesy flush. Where were we going, Santo Domingo, Dominican Republic? (If you are confused as to why I referenced Santo Domingo, book yourself on a flight from JFK to Santo Domingo — and back — and you will understand. It's unlike anything you have ever experienced in your entire life.) It was clear this flight delay was punishment. I firmly believe that passengers punish flight attendant by turning the lavatory into a war zone. That's the only explanation. Human beings waiting on an airplane for over an hour — and flying from JFK to Boston — should not act like they are barely surviving in Haiti after an earthquake.

"This lavatory is disgusting. What the hell is wrong with these animals?" I voiced to Mr. Coffee Stains hoping he'd get the hint to leave the galley; he did not. I reached around him for a pair of gloves, careful to avoid his mouth, and after putting them on, knelt down — careful not to touch the floor with my uniform — and cleaned up the lavatory floor. I expected it to stay clean for all of five minutes.

The Universe was looking out for me, or maybe it was just Melanie because once I was done mopping up other people's piss, the interphone rang and I picked it up instantly, "This is Joe."

Melanie spoke breathy, "Joe. There's an issue up here with the gate agent supervisor and a passenger. Can you come up here?"

"Sure. I'll be right there." I hung up the interphone and looked at Mr. Coffee Stains, "Can you watch the back doors for a moment while I go help her?"

"Yeah. No problem."

I quickly made my way up the aisle, avoiding the Russian lady, walking at a speed where I occasionally had to yell out, "Watch your arms." so not to plow into passengers hanging in the aisle.

Before I made it to the front galley, a guy seated at row four yelled out to me, "Hey man, what's going on? We're gonna miss our flight."

I stopped dead in my tracks and turned to my left. Sitting together in the 2x2 seat configuration was a hefty Bostonian and his equally sizeable girlfriend. Or wife. Or fiance. Or baby mama. Or all the above. I had no clue, but I put a smile on my face, "May I help you?"

The baby mama spoke up, "We've been sitting here for over a fucking hour. We're gonna miss our connecting flight. The flight attendant in the front can't seem to tell us anything."

The girlfriend did most of the talking, which was helpful because when the fat Bostonian guy attempted the English language, it sounded more like someone gargling marbles. Don't get me wrong, he tried to speak, but she continued cutting him off. She was crude and vulgar (my type of lady), but it was evident that she didn't make it through high school. If I had to guess, I'm sure she had a lower back tattoo.

I love New Englanders.

I beamed at her rudeness, "We're waiting on information from maintenance. We should be departing shortly."

"That's no fucking answer. That's what the pilot said an hour ago."

Boston guy stood up in the aisle, and I instantly curbed my attitude. He may have sounded like he suffered a brain injury, but this dude was tall and sturdy. Not the type of guy you mess with inside a metal tube. Let me rephrase that; he was the type of guy you fuck inside a metal tube, not fuck with. There's a difference. And by looking at this guy, I'd estimate it was a pretty big fucking difference.

I'd also like to note that I never flinched when she dropped the F-bomb on me twice. I gave myself a mental pat on the back for growing so much in the eight years I had been a flight attendant. I remembered the gate agent supervisor was only a few feet away in the front galley. Why the hell was I dealing with this bullshit? When the airplane is at the gate, and there is any passenger conflict, the responsibility falls on the gate agent. I am continually reminding myself of that specific policy. When I do, it's perfect timing. "Come with me, and you can speak to the gate agent.'

They followed me up to the front galley where I politely tapped the gate agent supervisor on the shoulder. She turned around with a scowl, which had zero effect on me, "These two passengers are going to miss their connection, and they are not happy."

Without another word, I made quick eye contact with Melanie, who looked like she was about to break down and cry, and spun around heading back to my galley. I figured dealing with the flight attendant who hadn't been in a dentist chair since puberty was easier to deal with than the Bostonian, his girlfriend, and that foul looking gate agent supervisor.

It just dawned on me, all these years later, that after getting distracted by the Bostonian and his girlfriend, I forgot to help Melanie with her original problem. I never realized that the Bostonian and his girl — who were an issue — weren't the issue that Melanie requested assistance with. At least I figured it out now, better late than never.

We still hadn't departed the gate, and it was starting to look like *Apocalypse Now* down the aisle of the airplane. In rapid succession, passengers continued walking to the back galley and asking me, "What's going on?"

I had no fucking clue. I was still in the dark as much as everyone else. On more than one occasion, I asked passengers to stand in the galley while I called Captain Mike on the interphone, "I have a few passengers here wondering when we are departing. Any clue?"

He gave his canned response, "No clue. We don't know anything."

How was that possible? The one thing keeping me from losing all control was that even with this lengthy delay, there was still a chance I'd catch my commute flight. As long as I had that to look forward too, I could handle anything else the airline threw at me on one of the most important days of my life.

If you have already forgotten, let me remind you — while I was dealing with this chaos and delay, only a few hours prior I had become a published author. Me, Joe Thomas,a changed man. Not just a small time blogger named Flight Attendant Joe, although that's fabulous enough, but Joe the published author. A goal of mine for decades had finally been achieved, and here I was, stuck in the back of an airplane — on a never-ending delay — being cursed at while cleaning up pissy toilet paper cemented to a lavatory floor.

Does J.K. Rowling deal with shit like that? I had no time to debate that idea because the sound of a call bell from my section snapped me back to reality. As I approached the well-dressed woman in 20B, I relaxed. "Hi, may I help you?" I asked leaning down towards her and shutting off the call bell at the same time.

A middle-aged, well-dressed woman looked up and smiled, "I just have to tell you, I've been watching you, and you are one of the nicest flight attendants I have ever experienced. You have stayed calm during this entire event. I'm impressed." With those kind words, she reached into her sizeable purse and handed me a box of fancy chocolates. It wasn't a big box — trust me, with the size of her bag it should have been a massive See's Candies box — but a small pink box which held four chocolates. It was just the right size to make my heart pitter patter and almost stop for a moment.

Kind gestures that come unexpectedly always throw me for a loop. It's the same with anal; I don't care what you say — you NEVER fully expect it.

I smiled at the chocolate lady, who ironically was black, "That's so nice of you. Can I get you anything?"

"No, honey. I'm fine. I just wish we'd hurry up and get out of here."

"I know," I answered holding onto my box of chocolates like it was a Pulitzer, "this delay is ridiculous. I hope you don't have a connection."

She giggled, "Yes, I do. And I will miss it. The sad part is that it's the second night in a row that you guys have caused me to miss my connection. Last night the flight was canceled and now today this."

Utterly embarrassed by the actions of my airline, I muttered out a pathetic, "I'm sorry," and followed it up with a hearty, "but thanks for the chocolates."

As I walked away, an older couple sitting behind the chocolate lady (I should honestly stop calling her that) stopped me, "Do you have a cell phone charger? Our phone is about to die, and we need to contact our daughter when we get to Boston."

I asked them to hold for a moment. I walked to the back galley, opened up my tote bag, and retrieved my cell phone battery charger. As I handed it to the wife with a smile, I added, "Do you have any chocolates?"

They stared at me so I quickly changed the subject, "Now don't take this with you or I'll have to chase you through the airport."

"You truly are the nicest flight attendant we've ever met."

In all the chaos from this delay, the idea that I published a book crept into my mind for short spurts, making me smile, but then a call bell would ring, or Captain Mike would call with more bad news, and my happiness would turn to reality. The reality that at that exact moment in time I was not a published author — and the master of my destiny — but only a flight attendant running up and down the narrow airplane aisle delivering a repeated message to the passengers.

Captain Mike finally came over the PA with information that the passengers, and flight attendants, were hungry for, "We have some great news. We will be departing shortly. Flight attendants prepare for departure."

It was as if Jesus Christ came over the loudspeaker and told every last one of us we were all going to Heaven (including that Russian bitch who deserved a slap upside the head with a herring).

After we departed JFK for our swift 45-minute flight to Boston, and conducting beverage service was seriously the last thing on my mind, the drama went from bad to fucking ridiculous. The interphone dinged with a call from Captain Mike. I quickly learned, after taking his calls while sitting at the gate, that Captain Mike delivered terrible news.

His wife probably kept her cell phone shut off most of the time.

He spoke first, "You know what, Joe, I'm putting you on my avoid list."

I responded, "I was thinking the same thing about you."

"We have additional bad news," he continued, "looks like the weather in Boston is so poor that we may have to divert to Hartford."

I stood in the back galley staring down the aisle knowing that if the airplane diverted to Hartford, all these desperate passengers worrying about catching their connecting flights would have to worry no more — they'd miss them, including my new friend who gave me chocolates.

"Mike!" I yelled, "You gotta be shitting me, right?"

"I wish I was. Let me call dispatch and see what's going on."

He hung up the interphone, and I spoke to Melanie who was in the front galley, "You doing okay?"

"I'm alright. This day is horrible. When will it end?"

I hung up and waited for Captain Mike to come over the intercom. A few moments passed before he addressed the passengers, "Ladies and gentlemen, we've got some more bad news. It looks like there's some nasty weather over Boston Logan and we won't be able to land there. We will be diverting to Hartford until we can depart and land safely at Boston."

I braced for the eruption from the passengers in the cabin, but it never came. That made me nervous. Were they planning a revolt? Were they plotting? I looked around for my box of chocolates, opened it, and tossed one back like a jello shot. If these people were preparing to strangle me with their headphones, they damn sure wouldn't be tasting my fabulous chocolates.

The interphone dinged again, and it was Captain Mike. As I picked up, I wondered if his next message was that we were ditching into the Connecticut River. It almost sounded easier than missing my commute flight, and at this point, I wouldn't be surprised if he wasn't doing all this to impress me for my phone number. "Okay kids, change in plans again, we are going to Providence. We shouldn't have to sit there long before the weather clears up in Boston."

My voice squeaked, "But I'm gonna miss that early commute."

"Sorry Joe, just not in the cards for you today. We'll be starting our descent down soon, prepare the cabin for landing."

As I hung up the interphone, Mr. Coffee Stains (remember him, the flight attendant whose teeth were the color of Turkish apricots) sashayed into the back galley, and I busted out a hearty laugh.

"What's so funny?"

"Oh nothing," I looked away so as not to wince at his teeth, "Just that this day can't possibly get any worse."

The urge to talk about my book bubbled up inside my throat choking me like an effervescent tablet. Each time my ego started peeking out, the Universe whacked it back into hiding. I needed to talk about something happy. Not diverting to Hartford (or was it Providence, I had already forgotten) but something that made me feel accomplished. Not a prisoner to stormy weather, Captain Mike, that Russian bitch, and the asshole who fueled the airplane wrong at the beginning of this nightmare flight. I honestly wanted to be with my husband and a few fans (I mean friends) while being pampered at a semi-fancy restaurant. I imagined popping expensive bottles of champagne and enjoying a glass or ten while my entourage praised my writing skills like, I don't know... Ernest Hemingway.

My ego is dangerous.

When we landed in Providence, the gate agents came onto the airplane and over the intercom asked any passengers if they wanted to deplane in Providence. Nobody took the offer.

It struck me odd that passengers were furious, exhausted, and ready to beat the hell out of the airline, but continued to be patient and almost kind to Melanie and I.

Every single one of us was frustrated. Stuck in Providence for an undetermined amount of time was not on the agenda. But here we were. The entire airplane full of passengers — and myself — missing connecting flights or flights home. We were in this together; me, Captain Mike, Melanie, Mr. Coffee Stains, and the 99 other passengers on the airplane.

After we departed for Boston, I sat on my jumpseat and accepted defeat. I missed my flight home, no reason to sugar coat it, and my only option was to deadhead back to Cleveland and make my way back home from there.

Then the interphone dinged. It was Captain Mike, but with a shocking twist. This time he had happier news, it was almost orgasmic, "Joe, I just called operations. I don't know if you realize this, but there is another flight to San Francisco tonight that leaves around 9:00 p.m. You will make that."

I wanted to jump through the interphone and give him a bear hug, "Thank you so much, Mike. I had no clue. Thanks for checking."

A flight that shouldn't last longer than 45 minutes was now pushing the four-hour mark. The most extended four hours of my entire flight attendant career. In the past, I had operated flights from Boston to San Diego that seemed shorter than this JFK to Boston hop. The moment the airplane blocked in at the gate, every passenger in the front half of the airplane jumped up and rushed towards Melanie. I disarmed my airplane doors and tried looking busy so not to make eye contact with any passengers. I quickly remembered that the older couple a few rows up still had my battery charger. I walked up to them, looked down at the wife, and she immediately announced, "Oh goodness, we almost forgot."

Let me confirm one thing, that bitch did not forget. While apologizing for the awkward Alzheimer's moment, she reached a wrinkled hand inside her purse for my $40 battery charger. I could understand, and forgive, her forgetting to return it, while it was stuffed in the seat back pocket, but stuffed in the bottom of her purse underneath her large bottle of Centrum Silver? Lovely try bitch, but I know your type.

When the last passengers walked off the airplane, I grabbed my belongings and raced to the front galley.

Melanie stood there pale with no more life left in her. "This has been the hardest day I've had at this job."

I hugged her and grinned, "It was great working with you. You are fantastic and not to scare you off, but you will have even harder days than this. Gotta go."

Captain Mike was already on the jet bridge as I stepped out of the airplane. I never stopped. I zoomed past him yelling out many thanks and probably even blew him a few kisses.

My departure flight was on the other side of the airport — it always is when you are trying to commute — and as I ran through the airport, I listed myself for the flight and checked in. Flight attendants are technically not allowed to use their cell phones while walking through the airport, but I considered this an emergency. I decided that if a flight attendant supervisor stopped me while I hustled through the airport, I would state that I was ovulating and needed to document it. Or something ridiculous like that. Listen, my airline picks from the bottom of the barrel to staff their supervisors, I figure they might believe it, some of them are about as bright as a bleached crayon.

I stopped in the restroom to do a quick costume change out of my uniform shirt and into a black polo shirt on the off chance my luck would provide me a seat in first class. I had my fingers and toes crossed. My shitty work day was enough, the idea of occupying a middle seat in the back of the airplane practically gave me a case of shingles.

My restroom stop paid off because when the gate agent handed me my boarding pass, it read 3C — first class. My atheist prayers answered, I ran down the jet bridge like an only child on Christmas Day.

I pulled my luggage onto the airplane, and after the lady standing in front of me moved down the aisle, I looked up into the galley and straight into the eyes of what I could only describe as an angel. My very own Teen Angel, but gay. My Gay Angel Jamie. The only way that moment would have felt gayer was if "It's Raining Men" by The Weather Girls started playing over the intercom while the two pilots — with their massive muscles and bulging pants — thrust themselves out of the flight deck and into me while passengers pushed past us to get to their seats. Everything wrong that happened all day quickly erased from my memory. Standing in the galley, with a wine glass in his hand and enough shade to cover Fire Island, was my longtime friend Jamie. We cheered, giggled, laughed, and hugged which cleared up any confusion that this was, in fact, a flight to San Francisco and not Montgomery, Alabama. If rainbows and glitter were ever going to fly out of my ass, it would have been at that moment.

"Well hello Mr. Published Author," he said, "Where are you sitting?"

After my manager, Garon, Jamie was the second person to acknowledge my achievement. I wanted to cry, but I also wanted to get into my seat and start drinking.

I smiled, "3C. Oh my god. I'm so glad you're working. This is amazing. I've had the worst day, but now I'm in first class, and you're here. It doesn't get any better.'

He laughed while mixing a drink for a passenger, "You had a bad day? I'm sorry to hear that."

"Yes. Diverted, delayed, and I didn't even know we had this flight to San Francisco."

"Well, don't worry about any of that. You will have a fabulous flight; I'll make sure of it."

It didn't take long to find my row and place my luggage in the overhead bin directly above my seat. I dug into my tote bag, pulled out my headphones and a few other essentials needed for the flight, and placed the tote bag next to my bulkier bag in the overhead bin. When I finally plopped down in my seat, that I knew would be flat with me passed out sleeping in the next few hours, I took enough deep breaths to calm my heart down from pounding inside my chest. I had made it. The celebration that I had waited for all day was about to commence.

After Jamie let the last few passengers onto the airplane and waited for them to walk down the aisle, he approached me in my seat, leaned in and quietly asked with a sly smirk, "Mr. Thomas, can we just go on record and say that all your drinks are doubles tonight?"

"That sounds perfect. It's on record."

The Universe, or whoever you worship, has no problem keeping your ego in check when you believe you deserve recognition for something.

It holds you down while you remain genuflected and screams, "Hold on, bitch, you ain't that important. You published a book, so what? Big deal, go clean that shitty lavatory."

On that remarkable day, I realized that life lesson quickly. I will never forget it. You are not as important as you think you are. There are billions of people just like you, doing the same things as you, all while getting kicked in the genitals by the Universe. But as much as the Universe bitch slapped me and rightfully put me in my place that afternoon, it now provided me with unlimited free first class cocktails for the rest of the night.

Journal Entry: Austin by way of Salt Lake City

Dear Journal,

I worked with two flight attendants I've known for a long time: Karen, who was called a racist by a passenger the last time I worked with her; and Benjamin Franklin. He's not the real Benjamin Franklin, but he might as well be. He looks exactly like Mr. Franklin. It's uncanny. He does. All he needs is a kite, string, and a key. I didn't name him Benjamin Franklin, Matt did. And everyone thinks I'm the evil one. Matt has sarcasm that makes me proud to be his husband.

The flight was delayed due to the weather. Airline management should eliminate their late occurrence codes for flight attendants and pilots because flights are rarely on time, and it has nothing to do with us. Once the airplane was on its final approach, we headed over to the terminal to get coffee before the aircraft landed. Mind you; it's 3:00 p.m. and I'd been up since 7:00 a.m. with no coffee. How I hadn't murdered an old lady in a wheelchair is a shock to me.

While standing at the gate with the racist — I mean, Karen — she excused herself to the restroom. I took a few sips of my coffee and decided to go to the toilet before the airplane arrived.

I walked into the men's restroom and smacked right into Karen. Almost spilled my coffee, which would have pissed me off for the rest of the night. We stared at each other like naked teenage siblings. I busted out laughing. I could never replicate the look of pure horror on her sweet Mormon face.

I asked her, "Why are you in the men's restroom?"

She couldn't speak. She created a new language standing there, "I. I. Um. Oh, my God. I don't. Oh, my. I don't."

If I were nice, I'd have moved out of the way, but I'm not that kind. I wanted to know why she was trolling the men's restroom. I knew she was in there by mistake, but it was fun to fuck around with the idea that she was actually in there looking for dick. It's like a straight Republican senator sucking dick in the handicapped accessible stall. When you witness it, you relish the moment. I said handicapped accessible stall because there's more room, and if anyone finds themselves in the restroom sucking dick, they need space.

When I moved over, Karen raced out of the restroom as if she had just given birth in the toilet. I walked in and saw a hot bearded guy at the urinal. One could only pray to Joseph Smith that he'd be on my flight.

Spoiler: he was not.

The flight was quiet on our way to Salt Lake City. There were about a dozen Mormon husbands on board, and I swear I've seen a couple of them at a Lady Gaga concert. Is there an underground gay Mormon diva group in Salt Lake City? It's highly possible. Maybe it was a Madonna concert. No. Madonna is too much for gay Mormons. It was probably the Britney Spears show in Las Vegas. Anyway, they were flaming homosexuals. How do their wives not realize they are gay? Denial should most certainly end when you catch your husband performing oral on your best friend's husband. These men were so gay that they sounded like a herd of Liberace's boarding the flight.

On our way back to Los Angeles, it was a different experience. A teenage cheerleading competition was taking place in Los Angeles, and we were the lucky ones to transport these future stay-at-home moms from Utah to California. As the lead flight attendant, I stood at the front of the airplane during boarding. They had ribbons in their hair, teddy bears in their arms, and most likely broken hymens between their legs. I only say that because they are cheerleaders and HELLO... I went to high school.

Most of these girls stepped onto the airplane in a panic. One of them, with a ribbon in her hair, declared, "I'm afraid to fly. This flight is my first time on an airplane."

I reassured her everything was safe. The next girl stepped on and followed up with, "I've flown many times. I'm not afraid of anything."

She most certainly had a broken hymen. Probably wasn't afraid of the football captain's fingers either. Behind them, I noticed an older blond woman on the jet bridge. She pulled a carry-on and had a handful of poster-sized cheer boards. What the fuck is a cheer board? I had no clue. After Karen explained it to me, I realized cheer boards don't matter. They make the world a terrible place. Large signs with words printed in bold: SCORE, WOW, GET IT. I have yelled those same words while watching a gangbang in the restroom at the New York City Eagle.

This cheer mom (cheer mom is an actual fucking term) stepped into the galley while staring me down like the Chipotle burrito she scarfed down for lunch. She scowled, "What should I do with these signs?"

The option of sticking them up her tight Salt Lake City ass was probably not an option. Scratch that, if her husband was a closeted gay man, I doubted her ass was tight. I offered to put them behind the last row of the airplane. Not really supposed to do that, but I'm a nice guy.

Her rebuttal came quick, "Can you put them in the closet? That's what they did last time."

She lost me. When a passenger says the words — last time — I shut down. This moment was this time, not last time, and my airline doesn't have closets.

I answered back, "We don't have closets."

Cheer Mom threw me a crippling death stare. If she were the Death Star, I'd be Alderaan. I wasn't afraid. I'm sure her husband wasn't either until she caught him watching gay sex videos on Xtube. I continued to smile, but I found her more annoying than hemorrhoids. She stomped down the aisle carrying her fuck boards (sorry, cheer boards), and I realized she was worse than the teenage cheerleaders. Before we closed the airplane door, I walked over to her and noticed the boards were slung all over the row. Cheer Mom was about to get cut. I finally, after a few minutes, convinced her to put them in the overhead bin on top of luggage pieces. She wasn't happy, but fuck her.

During the flight, the male passenger in 1E — who was wearing a feather earring — attempted to be flirtatious. It was not working. It's annoying. I warned him a few times that if he continued his behavior, I'd personally ban him from the airline. He ate up my sarcasm, which is the only thing he'd be eating up on the flight. My jokes were alright, I usually come up with better material, but I was still perturbed at Cheer Mom. I'm sure Feather Man wanted me, but I refuse to fuck someone who wears a feather earring. Even if it's an Indian Chief, who owns Hard Rock International.

When we landed, we rushed over to another gate to change airplanes. The gate agent watched us walk towards our new departing gate. As we approached, she shook her head in discontent, "Where have you guys been? We're running late?"

I caught my breath from dashing through the terminal, "Our original flight was delayed. And, we're on time, the airplane was late."

She peered at me for a brief second, shook her head again, and began typing on her computer. My ears and neck turned pink. I wanted to ram the baggage sizer up her ass. I'll never understand gate agents. We're all in this airline nightmare together. Karen, Benjamin Franklin, and I ran from one airplane to another, without the option of getting food, so the last thing we needed was some piss poor attitude from a gate agent. We get enough of that from the passengers; we don't need it from our coworkers, too. Save all that shitty attitude for your spouse and leave us flight attendants alone.

That felt great!

She handed me the manifest and demanded, "When will you be ready to board?"

Jesus, Mary, Joseph, and Madonna — settle down. I hadn't even walked on the airplane, done my security checks, or met the pilots. Maybe I'd be ready on; I don't know — November 17, 2022. The gate agent informed me that we had a passenger who needed a straight-back chair. Straight-back chairs are for passengers who should live in a nursing home, where the farthest they travel is to visit the flower garden at the far end of the property. Not on an airplane where the Earth must stop rotating for them to board.

That sounds terrible. I feel horrible for saying that. I don't mean all that; I was just frustrated and fucking hungry. Thankfully, the disabled passenger moved around like an energetic earthworm and was the most accessible straight-back passenger I've ever had. He looked like an actor from *The Middle*. I wonder if my friend Laura knows him? Maybe it was him; I'll never know.

We had two female pilots flying to Austin, which meant — no drama. Male pilots could learn something from female pilots. Female pilots have their shit together. Male pilots cry like their diapers are always filled with shit. And not typical shit, I'm talking sweet potato and corn shit. Baby shit. The shit you continue finding days after you cleaned up the baby. How male pilots fly airplanes without their wives helping is a mystery? These dudes act like such whiny babies inside the flight deck. I need this. We need that. My balls hurt. Flight attendants are bitches.

I guess that last one is true.

Right before boarding, our captain said, "We're going to fly the shit out of this airplane and get to Austin on time." Done! That was that. No need for an additional trash bag. No need for extra bottles of water. No need for brewing a cup of coffee before departure. No Diet Cokes with three cubes of ice. Not a damn thing.

Music lovers filled the airplane on our way to Austin. The couple in 2A and 2B had already been drinking at the airport before the flight. That was obvious. On our way to Austin, I served them each two vodkas, and they got obnoxious. I had to say, "Please don't stress me out," when they continued ordering drinks and acting like they were the only two on the airplane. They tipped me $8.00, so I guess they weren't that obnoxious. I paid everyone's tip for our hotel van ride — including the pilots — just for some additional useful karma.

That's when my patience began to run onion-skin thin. We landed on time at 1:20 a.m. and the hotel shuttle was scheduled to pick us up at 1:40 a.m. We waited outside, and my feet ached and burned. Did I mention I was exhausted? The moment we stepped out to the curb, a different airline canceled a flight to Las Vegas. All their passengers stood outside, screaming at the tops of their lungs, creating a wave of chaos that swept over us. I felt their pain, but did they have to be so irate around me? They could have taken all that noise to the other end of the airport, so I didn't have to hear it. No sound, just sleep. That was my motto for the night. I should have that printed on a t-shirt.

The hotel shuttle finally arrived at 2:20 a.m. You do the math — I was not happy. I refused to speak because I didn't want to start a scene like the stranded Las Vegas passengers. My silence was deafening to those around me. The driver was attractive, but that was lost to me once I realized he took the long way back to the hotel to avoid traffic. To be honest, I didn't see another car on the road for miles. We arrived at the hotel, and it was swarming with people at almost 3 a.m.. The front desk clerk was beyond stressed. When I got to my room, the key didn't work — a running theme with me at hotels, and something that only happens when I can barely put one foot in front of the other. I dragged myself back to the elevator and to the lobby to have my card re-whatever the fuck they do to cards when they don't work-coded and waited while the front desk clerk managed a large group of drunks. The drunks finally dispersed, he helped me, and I was back in the compact elevator headed to the tenth floor.

My head hit the pillow at 3:15 a.m. I set my alarm for 10 a.m. because rain was in the forecast and I wanted to explore Austin before that started. Right before I shut my light off, there was a knock at my door. Was it a drunk person or somebody lost? I had no clue. I opened it to find the attractive hotel van driver checking to make sure everything was acceptable. Did he expect a rapist in my room? Was he the rapist? My mind flooded with questions about why the hell he made house calls. Did he check on Karen? I doubted it; she'd have pulled him in. I hadn't forgotten her male restroom escape earlier that day. Did he check on Benjamin Franklin? No. Nobody checked on B. Franklin.

I assured him I was safe, comfortable — thanked him for his kindness — and closed the door. I wondered if he was looking for an invite. If so, he wasn't getting one; I was exhausted.

We All Need Balcony People Part 1/2

Initially, I had titled this chapter The End of Evan. It sounded perfect for where my heart, brain, and anger was at the time I sat down to retell this story. But thankfully my husband Matt, who controls his emotions better than I do, was there to guide me in the right direction.

After discussing the concept of this book with him, and explaining the outline, it only took him a few sentences to convince me to change the title, "Is Evan dead? No. So don't title the chapter that."

Here's the hard pill to swallow, although he's not dead, our friendship might as well be. Deader than Aunt Edna on top of that station wagon in *National Lampoon's Vacation*. Colder than North Dakota in the middle of January. Finished like Harvey Weinstein's career.

I think you get it; it's fucking done.

Part I

Evan was a prominent feature in my world for years. If my life were a television show, he'd have been a series regular. He was a leading star, but if there's one thing we know about stars, they eventually fade away.

How does a friendship you felt would last until the end of time (or at least until the end of your flight attendant career) end? I have repeatedly asked myself that question over and over again throughout this entire event. But the answer is simple; I was blind. I should have changed my name to Helen Keller. Helen was way more level headed than me. She had more insight than I do. Five minutes around Evan and I and she would have slapped us both in the face and said, "Don't you see what's happening?"

Or maybe not say, but finger doodle on our cheek. I think you get it. What I am saying is, I should have seen this head-on collision coming towards me from the beginning, I just never wanted to accept it fully. But it finally caught up with me in the summer of 2016.

This story started back in 2008. Our drama began when we first met, after flight attendant training, and after moving into the same crash pad together in Richmond Hill, Queens. It was a snowy day (of course it's a snowy day — it wouldn't be sunny and happy) inside a greasy Greek diner down the street from our crash pad. Evan and I were on late reserve call, so we bundled up and trekked through black snow for breakfast where we found ourselves sitting across from each other sipping coffee and downing pancakes and eggs.

"I just don't understand it. When will I find someone? I'm so tired of being single." He asked while squeezing half the bottle of syrup on his pancakes.

Putting my coffee cup down, "I don't know how you stay so skinny." He smiled, and I continued, "You'll meet someone when you least expect it. Stop looking. Be happy with yourself and then you'll find someone."

He shrugged, "I guess. I don't know. Ever since Albert, I don't think I'll ever find someone."

"Stop. Yes, you will. You are amazing and —"

He interrupted, "I mean… even you're married."

That stung as if a bee flew down my throat and drove its stinger straight into my heart. A comment like that coming from your best friend was like being shanked in the mess hall line by your prison nemesis while waiting for burnt toast and runny eggs. I looked it up on Google; a toilet paper shank is a real thing. I've got to hand it to prisoners; they are a creative bunch. All I do on the toilet is tweet angry messages to Donald Trump.

But this was Evan, a far cry from Donald Trump. For one, Evan knows how to read, write, and hasn't — or so I believe — ever gloated about grabbing a woman by her pussy. On the contrary, he'd probably run from one. The explanation was simple; I misunderstood him.

At that moment, I did what I believed the average person does when faced with truths they don't want to deal with; I ignored it. That's my MO. Instead of flinging my eggs at him and questioning his motives, I sat there tossing the eggs down my throat. I took his words in, thought about them for a brief moment — without allowing my facial expression to change — and placed his words in a little box I store all the life events that I don't have the balls to manage. I've been doing this for decades. I'm not saying it's healthy, or right, but it's the Joe way.

Am I the only one who is guilty of stuffing their emotional bullshit inside little boxes to deal with at a later date? If I am to be entirely truthful, that later date never arrives. I never deal with personal drama. My intentions start out good. I intend to man up and face the bullshit, but I rarely do. The circumstances are too much to bear. So I ignore it. And then before I know it, my emotional bullshit-stuffed small box is replaced with a trunk, then a walk-in closet. And when I believe I'm finally ready to tackle the issue head-on, I bulldoze head first into the issue, but by then it's the size of a large storage unit, so I turn around, close the door, place the padlock back on it, and say fuck it.

That's what this is all about. Not that my friendship with Evan ended, but how damaging it can be to ourselves, and the people around us, when we store all of our unaddressed bullshit inside little boxes and never have the nerve to pull it out and deal with it.

Evan's words, "…even you're married," planted a darkness inside my heart that never went away. Those three words left me wondering, did I deserve the love I found with Matt? Was it so hard for Evan to imagine someone marrying me? Was there a bigger question he was suggesting, who would marry a fat person like YOU? That's what my heart heard him say from across the table. His words didn't help that I was extremely overweight at the time, self-conscious, and struggled with looking professional in my uniform.

I knew I was fat; I didn't need my friend hinting that it was a mystery why I had a husband.

I packed his words inside one of my boxes (I am totally on a soapbox right now about these boxes) and even though it wasn't front and center in my mind, my feelings towards him began to fester like a cancerous tumor. In all the years we had been friends, each time Evan said something biting towards me I always remembered, "…even you're married."

There's no question in my mind that I blamed Evan for the negativity I carried in my heart. I accused him, but only partially. True, he said those words, but I allowed it. I never faced it and confronted him about it. I never questioned his intentions after his remark, and to this day, I still don't know what he meant. Did he think I was so disgusting that someone like me — fat, bald, no ass, big boobed, crooked nose — finding love before him was inconceivable? Without ever clarifying it with him, I had to assume that's what he meant. We should never take for granted the intentions of others, but I am never perfect, and I expected the worst.

The next speed bump in our friendship came in August 2012. When I say speed bump, I mean brick wall.

I had finished working a four-day pairing in Cleveland. During this time, Evan lived in Cleveland where I stayed at his apartment between work trips. We enjoyed each other's company, and I enjoyed not having to sleep in a filthy crash pad. In my two years crashing on his sofa, I can count on one hand the number of times I had to stay more than two nights in a row. The routine was always in one day, out the next, and then home as soon as possible.

Many times we wouldn't be at the apartment together. We either passed each other in the airport or more often, he'd be leaving his apartment as I arrived. But that particular night, we were both off work. With excitement, as I walked down the street towards his apartment, I pulled my luggage into the corner convenience store to buy a few bottles of cheap wine to enjoy while we debriefed on his sofa. It became a tradition that when we were both at his apartment, we'd revel in bitching about the airline, drinking wine, conversing, and ending the night watching Madonna's *Truth or Dare* or Katy Perry's *Piece of Me*.

Or he'd record silly videos of me and publish them on Vine.

It was the same week I had published an article on my blog entitled, "12 Steps On How To Order A Beverage On Your Next Flight". This blog post turned my blogging career around. The post that made me go from three followers — me, Matt, and his mother — to dozens and eventually thousands. It's not millions yet, but I still have all my body parts crossed for that milestone.

I arrived at his apartment, quickly showered, got into my pajamas, and went into the kitchen to crack open a well-deserved bottle of wine.

"Why haven't you opened one of these yet? You don't want any wine?" I yelled from the kitchen.

From the sofa, Evan responded, "I was waiting for you queen. Bring them glasses in here. We need to catch up."

I laughed, he always made me laugh when he talked. I poured out two full glasses, corked the bottle of red, grabbed both drinks, and headed down the long hallway past the bathroom and his bedroom. As I walked down the hall and started a conversation, I cheerfully stated, "Can we talk about this blog post I wrote that went viral? It's crazy amazing."

My foot stepped through the archway leading into the living room, and whether or not he realized his tone, he spit out, "Do we have to?"

Another shank from my best friend. He thrust that knife into me again, as if he patiently waited around the corner in the dark to surprise me. His retort almost made me spill the wine I was carrying, but I am a professional wine drinker, so nothing throws me off that bad. It did catch me off guard, no denying that, but I refused to let it show. I continued into the living room, handed him his glass of wine, and then proceeded to sit down on the other end of the sofa. The idea of throwing the wine in his face came to mind, but I didn't want to sleep outside that night, and as I said, professional wine drinkers don't waste wine. It's somewhere in the *Wino Handbook*; I think it goes something like, *Thou shalt not spilith the winith if thou not want thou ass kickdith…* or something insane like that.

Evan's legs were pulled up underneath him on the sofa. He flicked his hair back, like most gay men with long hair do — probably trying to make me feel sorry for being bald — took a sip of his wine, and changed the subject handing me his cell phone, "I want you to see this guy I think is cute. He's six feet tall, lives in New York City, and wants to hang out with me on my next layover."

Pulling out another stellar performance, I smiled and took the cell phone, "Oh he's hot. You should meet up with him."

"I don't know. This guy seems too hot for me."

"Why do you say that? You look like a fucking model. Just don't act crazy and you'll be fine."

He turned his body to face me with his glass barely touching his lips, "Are you saying I'm crazy."

"No. But you act it sometimes when it comes to boys."

He laughed. "Girl, you know me. I don't know why I get like that. Anyway, how was your trip?"

And that was that. When Evan first said, "Do we have to?" it burned, but I convinced myself for awhile that he was only joking. That had to be it. He was joking. What best friend delivers a blow like that when you are trying to share excitement about your achievements? But after we finished both bottles of wine, and laughed the night away, I laid on the sofa with my eyes wide open, and reality flooded the room keeping me awake. It could have been the street lights; I don't know. Something kept me awake, and whatever it was, it pushed me to realize that Evan was not joking. He was far from kidding; he was serious. He didn't want to talk about my blog or that blog post, and we never did.

When I got home after my next trip, I discussed what happened at Evan's apartment with Matt. Three days had passed since seeing Evan, but the feelings were still palpable. In that time, I had worked a three-day trip, commuted home, and remained utterly dumbfounded by his actions. I looked at my husband "Why would he say that? Why wouldn't he be happy for me about this?"

Without hesitation, he responded, "It's jealousy. He's jealous of you. Plain and simple.

"No. Evan is not jealous of me. It's not possible."

Matt leaned over hugging me, "Don't worry about it. Just remember what Melinda taught us in therapy."

I shook my head in agreement. In that instance, I was reminded of the time in elementary school when my mother, Irene, explained to me how to handle bullies. It was now Matt's turn. Matt, my strong emotionally sound husband, was now helping me manage my adult bullies. The same message delivered decades apart and presented in a completely different way. Matt's tactic was to remind me of valuable lessons we had both learned from our therapist. When I was eight, my mother delivered her message with a case of Bud Light. Sadly, I was too young to enjoy the beer. But no worries, she did. Irene was notorious for being able to put down a case of beer, throw me in the back seat, and head out to the package store to pick up another one. That was all on a Saturday afternoon. And all while not wearing seat belts.

How did any of us survive our childhoods?

Irene's message was simple. While she cracked open her 10th beer can, she slurred out, "Tell them little fucks to fuck off. Then give them the bird and run like fucking hell."

It's a full-time struggle not following my mother's teachings on a daily basis.

Matt and our therapist, Melinda, were incredible. By this time in 2012, we had been patients of Melinda for about three years. Therapy is the best thing I can recommend to anyone. If you haven't sought mental health treatment, go now. I feel bad for people who don't have a chance to experience the benefits of therapy. Well unless it's because they are a Scientologist, if that's the case, I don't feel bad. You've done that to yourself. If it's because you don't have insurance, I feel bad... and guilty.

Not only was Melinda our therapist, but she became an influential friend. I am not talking Facebook friend. I am talking going out to dinner and visiting her at her home, friend. That was a distinct line to come to, and eventually, we stopped seeing her for advice, and just accepted her as our Jewish Bubbie.

But one of the most important lessons she taught me while I was her patient — and that's why I am putting it in my book — is about "balcony people."

There are two types of people in your life: balcony people and non-balcony people.

If only Irene knew about balcony people, it would have saved an eight-year-old Joe from being chased down the street after flicking off the classroom bullies.

A balcony person can be anyone in your life. We all have balcony people in our lives, you probably just didn't know what to call them. Most likely, your spouse is one of your balcony people. Maybe it's your boyfriend, girlfriend, or afternoon trick. (Side note: if your trick is a balcony person, if you are single, I'd commit to marriage. If they're putting that much effort into you, they are a keeper.) Decent family members are great balcony people. A best friend. An acquaintance. Anyone. A balcony person's role in your life is simple: if life was a stage, they are the fans who cheer you on from the balcony. They are your cheerleaders. Did you realize we have cheerleaders in our lives and we don't even have to be decent at playing a sport?

Life is great.

A balcony person will pull all your friends together when you get promoted at work. They come to all your stand-up shows. They share your recently published book on their Facebook page and congratulate you for reaching a life goal. They encourage you to be great and push you to be better. Hopefully, you are a balcony person to your friends who return the favor as balcony people to you. Unfortunately, it doesn't always work out that way.

Here's another thing about balcony people: you can't make someone be your balcony person. If you attempt to force someone to be your balcony person, you will be left extremely disappointed. It's like getting someone to love you when they despise you. It's a losing battle. Would you want someone who only stays with you out of obligation? Would you want someone to act as a supportive balcony person when they don't give a shit about you?

Evan was not a balcony person. He might have been a balcony person for other people, but when it came to me, it felt like he wasn't even in my fucking theatre.

I peeked into one of my boxes of emotional avoidance, and it became clear that Evan would never be truly happy for my achievements. I was wrong to expect that or demand anything from him. As I said, you can't make someone happy or ecstatic for you. If they don't feel it, they don't feel it. Once that became clear, and it took some time, I realized I had to let all the animosity go; to take out the trash and put it in the dumpster. I am not calling Evan trash, just all the anger, and frustration.

Another thing that became clear was that we were moving down different paths. Whether Evan picked up on that, I have no idea, but I felt it in my heart. Once you feel betrayed or rejected by someone you care for, and who you feel like you supported throughout your friendship, it's hard to go back.

Even though I began to face my emotions about Evan, in the end — I did nothing about it. I did something worse than what I had perceived Evan to do; I went right back to my old ways. I packed up everything that was now clear in my head into one of my boxes and taped it up tight. I ignored it. It's difficult confessing that at certain times in your life, you are weak. We want to stand up for ourselves when people speak down to us., but when it came to Evan, my hands were tied. I tried to confront him, but somewhere along the way, while packing my emotions in one of those boxes, I unknowingly packed away my balls.

After all that, I moved all my newly ignored feelings from that tiny box into a medium-sized trunk.

Things with Evan ran their course for a few years. In early 2014, I helped my friend, Trick Daddy, move to Florida. Trick Daddy is a pilot at my airline and someone that I met while working a trip with Evan in 2012. He's straight, married, and has a kid — which defines 95% of all airline pilots. The three of us met after working a four day trip together back in October 2012. After the trip, Trick Daddy fell off the radar, as most coworkers do in the airline industry. Then in early 2013, we accidentally found each other on Facebook, again, as most coworkers do, and struck up a conversation. I distinctly remember the conversation because it was right after his dog passed away.

He sent me a text message via Facebook: *How did you handle the loss of your cat? This is killing me.*

I completely understood his pain. Only two months prior, Matt and I had made one of the most difficult decisions in our life, to put down our beloved cat, Lucy. All these years later, it still hurts. The only thing I could say to him was: *It will get easier. Remember the good times and know he's not hurting anymore.*

From that shared experience, we formed a bond. A friendship that neither one of us saw coming. Even to this day, I think it's fascinating how such a sad and life-changing event in both of our lives brought us together as friends. I wonder if his dog, Chase, and my Lucy are in

Heaven hanging out watching us from up above. That puts a smile on my face. But knowing Trick Daddy, I'm sure if it's Chase and Lucy, Chase is slapping the shit out of Lucy for being a smart ass... or some other wicked behavior she picked up from me.

In January 2014, Trick Daddy and his wife were moving to Florida. My role in this adventure was to drive one of their cars down to Florida — while he drove in the other car — and his wife and daughter followed a few days later by airplane.

When I told Evan, he looked at me like I opened all his Christmas presents a day early, "Why did he ask you?"

I was surprised, "I offered. He was moving and needed help with driving one of the cars."

"Yeah. I get that, but why ask you and not me?"

"I don't know. Because we're friends."

"We're friends, too."

I had to push back, "Queen. When's the last time you even talked to him?"

He avoided the question, and then shockingly stated, "It's like you stole my friend from me."

Let that sink in for a minute. A forty-something accused me of stealing a friend. What happened to the two of us being friends? I had no response. What do you say to someone who blames you for taking a friend away from them when they never did anything to establish a friendship? Call me crazy — and I know I am — but meeting a coworker on a four-day trip, hanging out with them a few nights, and then never making any attempts at building a friendship does not entitle you to tattoo the word FRIEND on them.

I could be wrong. I've been wrong many times before.

That incident was a big red flag. And no matter how big that red flag was, I was a bigger pussy, so I added it to my trunk and continued living my life. Quietly, and without verbally alerting Evan, I began distances myself from him.

We missed our annual vacation to celebrate being flight attendants in 2013, and when it came time to schedule one in 2014, we just skipped over it. By this time, Evan most certainly picked up on me being aloof, because he'd only slightly pressure me with a random text: *Come on. We've got to plan a trip.*

I'd respond: *Yeah. Let's talk about that soon.*

But soon never came.

By the fall of 2014, I transferred from Cleveland to Los Angeles. It had nothing to do with Evan and all to do with hating the commute. During my two years based in LAX (where I still hated the commute), and living in the Bay Area, I barely spent any time with Evan. I believe, from August 2014 until August 2015, I saw Evan twice. That was a considerable difference from multiple times per month.

When we went so long without hanging out together, the first thing I noticed was I did not miss him. We still texted almost daily, but there were no arrangements made on either side to interact or plan a visit.

Then one night, while he had a San Francisco layover, the two of us had a huge argument. It started on Castro Street. Brunch at Harvey's, followed by multiple drinks through the late morning and early afternoon while bar hopping up and down the street. It felt refreshing. We laughed. We carried on like teenage girls — something we did very well together — and things seemed to be falling back into place. That's what we needed, a jumpstart to get our friendship mojo back. Evan and Joe together again. Who needs trunks of emotional avoidance? We were back.

Or so I thought.

After we both drank way too much, Evan had a bright idea, "Let's get your car and drive to Napa."

I laughed, "What? We're drunk. We can't do that."

"Sure we can. We just get in the car and drive."

My first instinct was he was joking, but then I realized he was serious. "No. I'm not doing that. You're crazy. Can you imagine us going back to my house and saying, 'Hey Matt, we're driving to Napa to drink even more.' He'd freak. Don't be ridiculous, queen."

"You worry too much." He raised his voice. The alcohol was now in control, "You don't know how to have fun. You gotta liiiiiiiiive, Joe. You gotta just say fuck it and live."

That irritated me, "What the fuck are you talking about? You think I need to live? I live perfectly fine." We were standing outside the crew hotel in downtown San Francisco yelling at each other like angry lovers, "There's something wrong with you. Who the fuck drives drunk to Napa?"

"You always have an excuse. You just don't know how to live." He continued egging me on.

Did he want to fight? Were we about to throw punches? I hoped not. For one, he's much taller than me and would most likely beat my ass. I, on the other hand, was fatter and could just throw myself on him. Once I had him on the ground, then I could kick the shit out of him. Being the fat friend has its advantages. Fighting him ran through my head as we yelled and screamed at each other in front of the hotel lobby. Other guests walked in and out the sliding glass doors without flinching as if it was entirely reasonable to watch two screaming queens yelling at each other in the street. Like two heroin addicts fighting over the only tourniquet.

Livid and beyond frustrated, I walked off. I was drunk, slurring my words, and stumbling down Van Ness towards City Hall while yelling out to the Universe that my friendship with Evan was officially over.

Then I bumped into a hooker who tried picking me up.

"You okay, baby?" She said grabbing my arm and trying to swing. I'm glad she didn't swing too hard, she was about 100 pounds heavier than I was. "You need mama to fix your pain?"

I shit you not. This is completely true. When a big tittied, fat ass, heavy-set black hooker hits on you, you remember it. You also look for a pimp. I was safe, the pimp was nowhere around, or the guy was hiding well. I stopped on the corner and pulled my arm from her tight grip, "I'm gay, so you're barking up the wrong tree."

"Awww baby boy. You just need some fun."

"How about I buy you some food?"

I was enraged, had just ended a friendship, and was still willing to help out a hungry hooker. It says volumes about my character. Sure this hooker probably wanted to stuff white boy cock in her mouth — and not food — but when you proposition a gay man, you take what you can get.

Also, please never question my multitasking skills while drunk on the streets of San Francisco. I am a fucking pro.

"Oh baby, you be sweet like sugar."

"Tell my friend that."

She looked around, "Who?"

I started to cross the street, "Never mind. Are you hungry?"

She wrapped her big black mittens around my tiny white paws and walked me into the 7-Eleven on the corner.

The counter employee looked at me with sympathy, like I was just another sucker pulled into her trickery. I wanted to yell out, "She ain't getting no cock so chill the fuck out," but my focus was buying this bitch some food so I could continue back on the path of hatred I had for Evan.

"Get whatever you want," I said before realizing my mistake. What if Hooker Lady started buying up lottery tickets? And what if the counter guy was her pimp? What if this was a setup? What if their goal was to kidnap me and ship me off to Thailand to be a ladyboy? How much does that even pay? Probably not enough, I had to get out of this mess and home to my husband.

Thankfully, my irrational thoughts were merely that. Hooker Lady grabbed a small bag of Doritos and asked for a pack of cigarettes. When I eventually shared this story with some friends, they gave me so much shit for buying her the cigarettes. For supporting her smoking habit. One friend listed reasons why it was wrong for me to buy her the cigarettes.

I responded, "SHE IS A WHORE! A pack of Viceroy is the least of her worries."

When I finally got home that night, Matt was already asleep, and I passed out.

The next morning, I texted Evan to make sure he was alive. I imagined my hooker friend retraced my steps and found him alone and angry outside the hotel. And I hate to say it, but Evan is more the type to befriend a hooker, climb into the backseat of her pimp's car, and go on staff as her publicist. I am not that type. Remember, I don't know how to live.

We apologized for our aggression toward each other from the night before. I was brutally honest. I told him how immature and stupid it was even to entertain the idea of driving drunk to Napa. He agreed. I reassured him that I know how to live — and I live moderately well — and I want to continue living which is the reason I refused to drive drunk to Napa. He agreed. I told him that I have a partnership with my husband and being irresponsible is not fair to him. Again, he agreed. I felt powerful with my honesty. He hurt me, and I unloaded my emotions on him. You could say that I emptied about 1/4 of my trunk of emotional avoidance on him. Was this a turning point in our friendship? Would I now feel secure enough to confront him when he offended or hurt my feelings? Could I sweep away the eggshells that crunched under my feet when we interacted?

Not really.

In June 2015, I added more to my trunk of emotional avoidance, making it a walk-in closet.

During my time on the Standard Advisory Team (a group of working flight attendants who interact with management on behalf of their peers) at my airline, I trained to perform flight attendant interviews. It's the most fun activity I've had the opportunity to participate in at the airline. Our LAX base is the smallest, and management is always looking for additional flight attendants trained in interviewing to help out. When they ask you to pitch in and provide your services, you don't say no. You also don't decline when they remove you from a trip that you were supposed to fly, pay you for that trip, and put you up in a hotel for two nights to conduct the interviews. When my base manager sent me an email asking me to help with interviews for two days in June, I jumped at the chance.

With excitement, I sent Evan a text: *They asked me to conduct interviews in LAX. I'm excited.*

He responded: *I want to do interviews.*

The first thing I noticed was how he responded. Nothing positive. No, "Good for you," or, "Cool." If you hadn't picked up on that, I sure as fuck did. But I fought my bitchy impulses — it's so difficult at times — and texted him back as professionally as I could: *I'm based there, that's why they asked me.*

That's an accurate statement. No fake news, all truth. Evan's base was in Cleveland; mine was in Los Angeles. Yes, we were both trained to conduct interviews, but they invited me and not him because I WAS BASED THERE.

Then he texted back: *It's because you're special.*

That hit me with some hardcore reality. Was Matt correct? Were all these slights and snide remarks the result of jealousy? I hoped not, but it was starting to feel that way. Again, I didn't say anything, I put it out of my mind and went on with our friendship. The sad part is, those thoughts never really left me. They smoldered. But I couldn't see that coming until it was too late.

Our conversation didn't end there. A few minutes later, as if I never mentioned conducting interviews, I received more text messages from him complaining about being single. I forwent discussing anything about myself and focused giving him full attention. The eggshells laid out thick, and I was barefoot. I don't say that to be mean; it's just the truth. For years, I sat back listening to his moaning and groaning about life but never doing anything to fix it. I suggested therapy, self-help books, more therapy — ANY THERAPY — but as soon as the conversation got too uncomfortable, he'd end it. He would tell me, "I don't need therapy. You're my therapist."

I had to bring it up to Matt because my ill feelings for Evan were bubbling over. I felt guilty because I had still not expressed my frustrations. How the conversation was always brought back to his problems. How I was at the point where I felt uncomfortable bringing up exciting things about my own life. It was a one-way road, and it pointed at Evan. That was how I felt. When I discussed this with Matt, he calmly stated, "You can't save him, and you can't change him. You can only do so much for someone."

It became apparent that we had a superficial friendship. It was as if I walked into my walk-in closet of emotional avoidance and came face-to-face with Evan. He had been hiding in there the entire time. All my feelings laid out side by side like designer shoes. As I've gotten older, I find that it's crucial for me to have deep and meaningful friendships. Life goes by too fast to invest in relationships that are dead ends. In your twenties, you have all the time in the world to figure out your bonds with people, but in your 40's, the clock is ticking.

By March 2016, my friendship with Evan was hanging on by a string. We hardly saw each other and barely texted. I felt happier that way, but I never told him.

During that time, a career change was brewing in my life. With a heavy heart, I decided it was time to leave LAX and transfer back JFK. Eight years had passed since I was a flight attendant in JFK, but with a dreadful schedule in LAX, the thought of commuting across the country seemed smarter than staying in a base where my seniority made me feel like a new hire. After eight years as a flight attendant, requesting a Thursday off for a doctor's appointment should not be denied. Not at my airline anyway. I hated commuting with a passion, but better seniority bewitched me.

Before I put in my transfer, I told Evan my plan. A few months prior, he had moved back to Queens from Cleveland. The fun memories we shared still lingered in my head, and I became excited with the thought of us being back together again in JFK. Months and months had passed since our last negative interaction, and during that time frame, I hadn't had to place anything inside my emotionally cluttered walk-in closet of avoidance, so I forgot all that was in there. It sat untouched and probably needed a few bottles of Febreze. I hate to admit it, but my emotions stink like shit.

I ignored my past emotions and thought we might be able to rekindle our friendship. So without reasoning, I sent Evan a text: *Hey. I'm transferring back to JFK in May. I can't wait to hang out.*

He immediately responded: *YES. OMG. It's going to be like old times.*

That was reassuring. I responded: *Can I get the number of the crash pad place you stayed at before you moved back to the city?*

He shot back a text: *Don't be crazy. You will stay with me again.*

Let me just say that sentence did not make me feel comfortable. There was no way I was going to go from seeing him twice in a year — and having all this unfinished business — to using his apartment as a crash pad. That was fucking absurd. The idea sat in my stomach like a brick while I stared at my phone thinking of the best response. I went the diplomatic route: *No. I don't want to put you out. Especially since you just moved back to NYC.*

He didn't hear any of it: *No way. I can't imagine you being here and not staying with me.*

I didn't know what to do, so I did what came natural, I caved: *Ok. I don't think I will be there that often. And I am paying you.*

That was in March. When May rolled around, and I was back in JFK, I went the entire month without needing to spend the night at his apartment. My seniority was finally in its rightful place where I was able to bid commutable trips (when you fly to the airport and work a flight that same day). There were a few nights I ended late in the evening, but I slept in the crew lounge on a lumpy sofa and caught the first flight home in the morning. It worked out flawlessly, but I had yet to spend any quality time with Evan. By the end of May, I hadn't seen him once. I figured if we were going to bring life back to our friendship, it was time to plan another vacation.

I reached out and suggested a trip to Cartagena, Colombia and Mexico City, Mexico. Three days in each. It's been a dream of mine to visit Cartagena — ever since watching *Romancing The Stone* — and Evan wanted to hit the streets of Mexico City. One thing about us when we head out on an adventure, we always get the most bang for our buck, and that usually included a multi-city stop.

As we texted details back and forth regarding the trip, we decided to schedule our travels for the end of July. It was a go, and I felt confident we needed this adventure to get us back on track. While all this went on, other stuff was happening behind the scenes. Specifically, the release of my first book, *Fasten Your Seat Belts And Eat Your Fucking Nuts.*

My manager, Garon, had scheduled me for the Out-Write Book Festival in Washington DC to read live during the first weekend of August. The idea kept me on cloud nine for weeks. Reading my book in front of people who came there to see me live? You could have pinched me, and I still wouldn't have woken up. There was a small problem though, it was June, I was scheduled to appear at the book festival in August, and I had yet to publish my book. It was a time crunch like I had never experienced. I had to finish the book, have my editor read it, fix the edits, get the artist to draw the cover, get the graphic designer — who lived in Barcelona — to do the front and back cover AND finally have it published.

I had no idea how complicated it was to publish a book. The walls were closing in on me. I felt swamped, and after reviewing my calendar, I realized there was no possible way I'd be able to do all this and go to Colombia and Mexico. No possible way. I was stressed and didn't want to discuss it with Evan. How would he take me canceling the plans? I imagined not very well.

Matt gave me a nudge and said, "Just tell him what's going on. He'll understand."

I resolved not to cancel the entire trip. I texted Evan: *Hey. I have to ask you a favor. Can we do Cartagena at the end of July and do Mexico City in September? It will help me out with getting this book done. I hope you aren't mad at me.*

He responded: *GURL. I'm not mad at you. I thought you were upset with me because we haven't talked more about the trip since the beginning. It's all ok and understandable with your book. If you want we can just do the whole thing in September.*

I felt this wave of relief and love for Evan. A feeling I hadn't felt in many years. Was he finally being the balcony person I had always wanted him to be? The friend that I needed him to be? It seemed real: *You're so amazing. That would be such a relief right now. I was stressing because I didn't want to upset you.*

I updated Matt, "He's okay with it. We're doing the entire trip in September."

Matt looked up from his laptop, "See. I told you. You just have to talk to people. And stop texting him all the time. That's no way to have a conversation."

Everything between Evan and I seemed right. Things had worked themselves out. Around June 10, our July schedules published. I quickly noticed that I needed to crash at his place for a few nights. I sent him a text message letting him know I needed to stay at his apartment. I didn't ask outright — totally my mistake — but I figured he'd just tell me when and where to pick up my key to get into his apartment. That was the arrangement in Cleveland, so I assumed the same for JFK. Never assume. That's a lesson I believe I will never learn. He responded: *What days?*

I told him the days I'd be there — those days are lost to me at this time — and his response went something like: *I'm working those days.*

That caught me by surprise. Why did that matter? That response made no sense. It might have made sense if I had not spent years staying at his apartment alone in

Cleveland, but that was not the case. I had a key and spent numerous nights alone in the Cleveland apartment. Did he not trust me? Did he think I would steal his flat screen television like he claimed I took our friend Trick Daddy? I had no clue what was going on in his head, and because I was a chicken shit, I didn't ask.

For the next few hours, we went back and forth texting while I questioned him about letting me stay at his place during those specific nights, but he continued dodging the question. Our conversation started fizzling out, and I still had no lodging between trips. When I realized I wasn't getting anywhere with him, I finally texted: *If I can't stay with you then can I have the number to the crash pad?*

He came back fast: *I already texted her, and she doesn't have anything available.*

What the fuck was happening? Sabotaged by my friend, that's what was happening. He had specifically told me months prior, as I have already shared, that I did not need a crash pad because I could stay with him. And now that I was cashing in on his offer, I was being made to jump through hoops. I am fat. I can barely jump rope, so fuck jumping through hoops. Was he doing all this on purpose? I had no proof, but my gut instinct at that very moment told me the entire turn of events was a calculated plot.

It made me sick to my stomach, and my walk-in closet of emotional avoidance instantly became a storage unit.

I shot back: *Well I need to find a place to stay and the hotels are too expensive.*

Like a kick in the gut, I looked at my phone, and these words danced across the screen: *Just book yourself on a Santiago red-eye flight and sleep on the airplane.*

I stared at my phone for at least two hours. That's an exaggeration, but it felt like hours. My friend had betrayed me. No question in my mind. Nothing anyone says, including him, could ever make me see differently. Perception is everything. After I collected my thoughts, I did the worst thing ever... nothing. I never confronted him. The only difference this time was I left the door open to my emotionally cluttered storage unit of avoidance so I could smell the hot burning embers of our friendship smolder. I never closed the door again. It's still partially open today. I held onto that anger to guide me through what would become a mentally draining conflict.

And a mentally draining conflict it became.

We All Need Balcony People Part II

After Evan suggested I sleep on an airplane I never responded to him, but I did the immature thing: I told mutual friends what happened. I started every conversation with, "Guess what Evan said to me?"

During brunch in San Francisco one morning, I shared the events with my friend Jamie. All he could do was shake his head and say, "Wow. Does he hate you? Santiago? Not even San Diego but Santiago?"

My actions were not the adult thing to do. It was pretty childish, but it felt right while I was doing it. To be honest, I didn't do it to make Evan look bad. That was just a side effect. I did it to validate my feelings of being wronged. That validation was important to me. It fueled my anger. I needed people on my side, soldiers standing beside me ready for a war I created in my mind. War I was fighting alone because I never had the balls to invite Evan to armor up. Again, not mature. Slightly embarrassing. If I could go back, I'd bitch slap myself two black eyes and a bloody lip.

I share responsibility for the demise of our friendship. I should have confronted Evan at that moment, and not on text but, like my husband suggested, on the phone. I should have called him at that very instant and said, "Sleep on a goddamn airplane? Who says that?"

This interaction made me realize our friendship was over. Severed beyond repair. Friends don't set their friends up for failure, and by failure, I mean encouraging them not to find a crash pad, because they say you can stay at their apartment, and then not allowing you to stay with them. All the years of him being a snarky bitch to me — and my sweeping it under the rug — had finally come to a head. It was like a volcano exploding inside of me. I hated him. I hated him more than anyone... than anything. I hated him more than being on reserve.

But I had yet to tell him. What seemed like a few weeks later, he texted me out of the blue: *Why so quiet? What are you doing? When are you going to stay with me in NY?*

Was he playing mind games with me? Did he graduate from the same mind fuck school my mother attended? With a text like that, I figured he was valedictorian. I thought long and hard about my response. Then I said screw it and opened the floodgates. I had zero fucks to give and nothing to lose: *Hey. I won't need to stay with you in NY. I got a hotbed crash pad, and I can sleep in the airport. After you told me to sleep on the airplane, I've decided not to stay with you at your apartment.*

Again, let me emphasis that this was all happening over text message. Big mistake. Huge mistake. I channel my inner Julia Roberts from *Pretty Woman* when I say that out loud. If you take anything away from this story and learn from my gaffes in life, let it be never to end a friendship over text message. You will regret it for years to come. Trust me, I am telling you from experience. It's stupid, childish, and unnecessary. Pick up the phone and call the person even if it's an awkward conversation. Do it. The friendship will most likely still be over, but you will have handled it the right way. I have read, *Crucial Conversations* and *Crucial Confrontations*, two books that prepare you for these types of scenarios, and I still wasn't man enough to call up one of my best friends and discuss this entire thing like adults.

He answered: *Queen. That was a joke for that one* night. *All the other nights were okay. Is this why you've been giving me the silent treatment?*

I knew we had to talk, but I was not ready, and I had no interest in talking to him on the phone. I continued to text: *We have some stuff to talk about, but I don't want to talk about it over text. My feelings were hurt. We'll chat soon.*

He shot back: *Sorry your feelings were hurt. It was a joke. Anyhoo.*

When I read that, I almost threw my phone across the room. Anyhoo? Anyhoo? That's Evan's way of saying — whatever. That's how Evan ends a conversation when he has nothing left to say about the matter. And I don't know what type of apology that was, but saying, "Sorry for your feelings…" does not take responsibility for being a dick. What he was saying was, "Sorry you can't handle what I said to you." That's not an apology.

An apology like that deserves a RAM truck shoved up your ass.

From his reaction, he probably assumed it wasn't a big deal and that I was blowing it out of proportion. And maybe I was, but I didn't think so. He told me to SLEEP ON A FUCKING AIRPLANE! I think my proportions were justified.

But let me play devil's advocate for a moment. In his mind, this was a one-off thing. I never shared my feelings and frustrations with him. He had no idea. The hostility and anger I had towards him had been building up inside me for years. The sleeping on an airplane comment naturally ignited it, but the fuse had been lite in 2008. In my mind, this was over eight years of comments that I had sequestered away finally coming to a head.

I stopped texting him after his "anyhoo" comment. I had nothing to say. I saved it on my phone though — as an unfriendly reminder. He'd send me random text messages once in awhile, and I would answer with short responses. I didn't want to talk to him. I wasn't ready to call him. Would I ever be ready? It wasn't looking like it.

Matt asked, "How're things with Evan? Have you guys talked this out yet?"

I got nasty with Matt, "I'll talk to him when I'm ready. I'm not ready yet. I may never be ready."

That went on for a few weeks. I was not ready to deal with Evan, so I ignored him. I checked out of the friendship. It was the end of Evan. When I assumed our friendship wouldn't survive, I erased pictures of us off my phone and deleted him off Facebook.

Yes, I said it. I deleted Evan from my Facebook page. Do you want to know how to bring attention to yourself when you are having issues with a friend? Delete them from Facebook without warning.

Childish? Yes. Immature? Yes. Unnecessary? Completely. I have already confessed that I am also guilty of the death of our friendship.

To be honest, I did it without thinking. I can't even begin to remember why I chose to delete him from Facebook at that specific time or date, but I did. I will blame temporary insanity and loss of any critical thinking skills. I opened up my laptop, pulled up his name, and hit delete. Not a moment of hesitation or regret.

Facebook asked, Are you sure? At that moment, I damn sure was.

His text message came shortly after: *Daaaamn, so instead of talking about how you honestly felt about the silly Santiago comment, you unfriend me on Facebook.*

He was forcing me to discuss this with him, but still, nobody picked up the phone: *I wanted to talk to you and not via text, but you said anyhoo… which we all know, means you don't wanna talk about something. I did delete you on Facebook but I was upset and emotional, and it was a childish move. If we are gonna talk it should be on the phone and not via text.*

An hour later he sent this: *It was a serious and childish move. I get you were stressed about finding a place to stay for a night because I was working and not available, which is why I jokingly mentioned booking a red-eye flight. I have to say, Joe, we didn't have the friendship I thought we did.*

I refused to believe Evan was only joking because I actually slept in the airport. Then I had to fly to Orlando, rent a car, and stay with a friend because hotels were too expensive by the airport and the hotbed crash pad was full. It wasn't a joke. A joke text would have been: *Sleep on an airplane. HAHA Just kidding.* There was none of that.

Then I got angry: *Our friendship was severed the day you told me to sleep on a fucking airplane. I owned up to being childish for deleting you on Facebook, yet you still haven't said the words, "I am sorry," about something that has ultimately been the catalyst to end our friendship.*

Evan wanted to have the last word in this argument; I couldn't blame him: *You are psychotic. YOU are the catalyst that ended our friendship because YOU took it upon yourself to end things without even telling me how you felt about the stupid red-eye comment. And for the record, I did say I was sorry that your feelings were hurt and that my comment was just a joke, but judging by your actions it seems deeper than that... like San Andreas deeper. It's a mystery to me because you haven't ever expressed your dislike of me or our friendship. No need to respond, thank you.*

My friendship with Evan was over. I sat on that for a few days. I cried. I thought about us at the airport on vacation in Helsinki, Finland, me freaking out about getting stuck there, and him calmly snacking on almonds, perched on top of his suitcase, telling me to calm down. All that was over. It was hard to swallow.

Two weeks went by, and I started questioning if I made the correct decision with Evan. Eight years is a long time to take a friendship to the curb and let a sanitation worker take it away. I was confused and continued bringing it up to Matt.

"What do I do? I don't know if it was the right thing ending the friendship?"

"You followed your instinct. You told me that the friendship hadn't been the same in years. If you felt like it was over and Evan wasn't a good friend to you, then you did the right thing."

I agreed. I didn't believe Evan had been a lousy friend, but I wouldn't say he had been the best friend. He was not a balcony person, but maybe he was never meant to be one. I didn't know what to do, but then one afternoon I was cleaning house and decided to send him a message.

Instead of texting, I went up a notch and left him a voice message on an app. I figured that was better than a cold call without giving him the heads up.

My voice message was playful but apologetic (even though he had never sincerely apologized for the sleeping on an airplane comment). The short version of the voice message was: I asked him that if there was any way we could resolve our differences and move forward with our friendship, he was free to call me so we could clear everything up. I was wrong. He was wrong, so let's fix it.

The next day I received another text message: *I appreciate you reaching out. However, I don't know what to say. Ok, I do have to say I felt you sabotaged our friendship over an innocent and stupid comment. I felt blindsided because of how quickly and quietly you cut me out of your life which, sadly, makes me think our friendship wasn't that meaningful to you. Again, I appreciate you taking the time to reach out. I don't think we can put a band-aid on this and be ok.*

And with that, the chapter closed on our eight-year friendship.

Journal Entry:
Shit Happens

Dear Journal,

Justin drove up to LA from San Diego to hang out with me for the night, and there was no time to waste. After I checked into the hotel, showered, and changed, we hopped in an Uber and headed over to a bar/restaurant where we survived a *Sister Act* sing along. Holy shit, it was painful. These queens made Whoopi Goldberg sound like Jennifer Hudson. On a positive note, the bartender Benny was hot. Big, hairy, and wearing a t-shirt that said, "Size Matters" which we all know is correct. I don't care what anyone says. Size matters, and not just when shopping for boats and RVs.

I told Justin I'd let this guy do things to me that were illegal in Alabama and he quickly reminded me that on my birthday, a few years prior, I confessed my rape fantasy. Not just rape, but the desire to be beaten up and left for dead. There, I said it. Feels good writing it down. Would I go through with it or search it out? Probably not. That's why it's a fantasy, and honestly, I don't think that's how rape works. It's usually not planned.

We bar hopped and then, without warning, my sphincter started screaming. And not for dick. I had to shit. Why does this happen to me when I am at a bar? Fucking potstickers, chicken tenders, and nachos from dinner were coming back around to show me *Who's The Boss*. My asshole was Tony Danza. Or was it Angela Bower? I can never remember who was the real boss. But seriously, I don't fool around when it comes to shitting. I have a three-minute window. From the moment I realize I have to deuce, the clock starts ticking towards my emergency evacuation. I've shit myself more than a newborn, so I don't take any of this lightly.

The last time I shat myself, Matt and I were on a hike. It was a while back. Alright, it was last week. I'm sorry, I couldn't hold it. Don't judge. Maybe I need to see a specialist. A proctologist would be nice. Then I'd get fingered, and he could explain why I shit myself more often than an Alzheimer's patient on a field trip to the mall.

Nothing says cathartic like writing your most embarrassing moments down.

We still had over a mile to go before civilization. I unloaded my bowels under a lone tree next to a concrete block. I felt like an animal. Or at least a drunk. For sure a homeless person in San Francisco. Matt continued walking while I made animal sounds and ended up burying my underwear under the tree. I hope it never grows. That would be a shitty tree.

When I ran up to him, without wearing underwear, he said, "I have to use the bathroom… like a human being."

All I'm going to say is, he knew what he was getting into when he married me.

The gay bar Justin and I were at had no doors on the restroom stalls. Why does that happen? Who just plops a fucking toilet in the middle of the restroom and says, "That's a wrap. Let's open for business." There was a turtle playing peek-a-boo through my back door, and I had to think fast. Chocolate turtles are nothing like chocolate Easter bunnies; I promise you that.

The bar down the street had a private restroom, so I told Justin to hold my beer while I sprinted the two blocks to destroy the porcelain. Lava poured out of me like I was dying. If I were standing in the Pacific, I'd have started my own Hawaiian Island. What would I name my creation? Joeaui? The Big Joe? Joeahu?

It ought to be Joeahu. That's perfect. I don't know about you, but I'd live there. My moans were muffled by the dance music shaking the walls. That was a plus. Some asshole banged on the door which frightened more shit out of me which caused another eruption. As you can tell, I am not shy about shitting in a bar. Some queens would never shit in a bar. They wouldn't even shit three miles from the bar. They'd cause internal damage to their organs before pulling down their pants to shit at a dance club.

Not me. Honestly, it's not even my first time.

In my early 20's, I did the unspeakable. I can't believe I am writing this down, but I feel it's time to face my past. My husband won't even let me share this shit story. When I attempt, he runs out of the room. I try reminding him it's only shit talk and I'm not actually taking a shit on the coffee table. I think he's confused. But then again, he's one of those people who acts like a fart never happened. No matter how stinky. I've tried breaking him of this behavior and making him giggle or laugh when he hears a fart, but he forces himself not to smile.

I expect that's how he's going to die. Not from farting, but holding back the childish behavior that comes with a big juicy one.

It was 1991. Or maybe 1992. It was 1992. Or 1991. It was one of those years, hell if I remember. I had gone out to The Parliament House in Orlando, Florida. It's probably one of the most popular gay bars in the country. If you don't know about the P House, you are either Republican or brain dead.

I was out drinking with a few people. One being my best friend, Gary Jones, and a few of his coworkers. Before we went out for drinks, we stopped at a restaurant for dinner; I had chicken wings. Who goes out for chicken wings before going to a gay bar? Nobody warned me not to have chicken wings. I hadn't yet memorized all the rules of being a homosexual, and I felt like I was out on my own. I was also a virgin, so I had no clue that chicken wings should not come into play when the possibility of anal might be on the table. Bad gay. For me, anal wasn't an option, because the only thing getting anywhere near my ass in 1991/1992 was toilet paper. After downing my chicken wings, we headed out for drinks and dancing at the club. Everything was going fine until the last few minutes before the bar closed. It was around 1:50 a.m. when it hit.

Jesus Christ, it sounds like I'm retelling a story about Hurricane Andrew.

My stomach started to rumble like the 1989 San Francisco Earthquake. I wasn't actually in San Francisco at the time, but I can imagine that's how the ground shook. I didn't know what to do; I started to panic. When I saw my party walking towards me, I told them I had to run to the restroom. They said they'd wait for me outside and I didn't let on what was happening. I figured I'd take care of my business, and nobody would be the wiser.

That was not the case. I stepped into the restroom, and there was a line of guys waiting for the two urinals and one toilet available. There was no door on the stall for the toilet, just a half wall that protected it from any onlookers. THAT WAS IT! I stood behind a few guys and leaned against the wall. I switched back and forth from one foot to the other. I played it off like I was dancing to the music. It worked. Nobody thought anything until the toilet became available and I ran to it like my asshole was on fire.

Nothing like this had ever happened before. I had to evacuate my bowels to the point that I didn't care if I was on a live feed broadcast for everyone on the dancefloor to see. Let them watch me shit while they danced around to "Baby Got Back". They had no clue that Sir Shits-A-Lot was making his remixes a few feet away. I pulled my pants down, and without warning, my asshole exploded. Literally. EXPLODED. When it erupted, I sat down and slid off the seat. I grabbed the handles and let every possible animalistic sound escape my body. If there had been a door on the stall, people would have thought a rhino and lion were fucking. I'd have frightened the Indominus Rex while on vacation at *Jurassic World*. Sweat cascaded down my face like I was doing hot yoga on Mercury. I wanted to wipe it away but stopped myself because I was pretty sure I had shit on my hands.

It kept coming out of me. There was no sign of it stopping. What were in those chicken wings? Ex-Lax? I figured they'd close the bar and I'd still be giving birth to the Antichrist. Because of the half wall blocking my face from view, I didn't have to make eye contact with anyone. That's how I've been able to show my face in that bar again. Black tile covered the restroom walls, so it was easy to make out people's bodies while they stood up against the wall. The sweat and shit continued to pour, and I wanted to flush myself down the toilet.

It took awhile to clean up. I won't go into details, but it was a shit bomb. If ISIS used suicide shit bombers, I'd have been their first recruit.

I waited until the restroom was empty. I stuffed toilet paper into my underwear, pulled up my khaki shorts, and walked over to the basin to wash my hands. As I was scrubbing the shit from my hands (yes, there was shit on my hands) Gary's friend, Brian, walked in. I remained calm but prayed he didn't walk to the stall.

He walked directly to the stall. I am not shitting you, straight to my stall.

Did I just write, I am not shitting you? Hilarious.

We didn't exchange words. I quickly dried my hands and walked out meeting up with the other two in my group. I remained steady and calm. I wasn't going to give myself away. A few minutes later, Brian walked outside. He sauntered right up to me, looked dead in my face and said, "Damn. Did you see that nasty shit someone took? People are disgusting."

I agreed and fought back the tears. We jumped in the car and drove away. We stopped at a 7-Eleven for gas, and I had to shit again. It was at this stop, while I was in the restroom, that I noticed my khaki shorts had a long banana shaped shit stain going down the back. Had anyone noticed? Was I found out? If I were suicidal, this would have been a great time to end my life. I threw my underwear in the trash can, pulled my shirt out to cover my shit stain, and left the restroom.

In the car, Gary and I dropped off the other two at Brian's apartment and drove away. We pulled up to a red light, and without being questioned, I screamed, "IT WAS ME. I SHIT IN THE BAR. IT WAS MEEEEEEE!"

And that's my shit story. The one Matt never wants to hear.

Let me get back to Justin in Los Angeles. I swear, I'm all over the place with my shit stories. I have way too many of them. Growing up, I never thought I'd be the guy with too many shit stories.

When I got back to the other bar, Justin was surrounded by young thugs. A Mexican entourage. He's like Jeannie from *I Dream of Jeannie*. He folds his arms, nods his head forward, and uncut cock appears. He believes it's a gift. I think it's the reason I'm always checking for my wallet when we are at a bar together.

One of the guys standing around him was pleasant, one was polite, and one I did not like. There's always one in the bunch, and I will unceasingly find them. I can't help it; I am not a fan of strangers. I'm a prisoner to first impressions, and if we don't hit it off, I'll talk to someone else. The guy I did not like was unfriendly to me, but when I'd walk away to get another beer, he'd tell Justin I was hot. It's junior high school, but with adults. Anyway, he wasn't my type, but there was a taller guy who had a nice look. From far away that is, up close he looked like his parents were siblings. Not that I have anything against that look, it's just not my thing. First cousins — maybe — brother and sister parents, NO! I have to draw the line somewhere.

Even with a solid chance that his parents were twins, I followed him into the restroom. After he finished pissing, he blocked the door, pulled out a bottle of Febreze, and started Febrezing himself. Everyone is a freak. I stared ahead while peeing because I didn't want to disturb him. I hoped this wasn't a ritual he performed before raping and dismembering a stranger. Yes, I have a rape fantasy, but it doesn't include a dirty bar restroom with a guy who smells like my apartment before my party guests arrive. Mr. Febreze told me he was a smoker and hated the smell of cancer on his clothes. After that, I was ready for bed. Alone.

The Uber ride back to the hotel was entertaining because our driver was Middle Eastern and hot, but I wished I had grabbed that bottle of Febreze. The smell of stank armpits and lack of soap scorched my nose hair. Justin talked him into stopping for doughnuts which were definitely not what my chubby ass needed before bed.

Thankfully, I survived my evening of drinking, but the moment we arrived at the hotel, I went to the bathroom and became curious whether I shit myself at the bar. Did I make it in time to the toilet? Was I that drunk that I fabricated the entire story in my head?

No, I made it to the restroom. Unfortunately, my underwear told an entirely different story. My briefs resembled a race track at the Daytona 500 after a five car pile up.

Drunk, Disabled, or Medicated?

As we stood at the gate awaiting the airplane's arrival, Carla, the lead flight attendant, walked up to me and whispered, "We have six wheelchairs on this flight."

"Six wheelchairs? Going to Vegas? Jesus Christ," I responded not breaking the gaze from my cell phone, "I can picture them all lined up at the slot machines, not able to walk, but able to smoke and gamble."

She continued, "And the wheelchair employee just told me that when she picked up a passenger from the bar, he appeared drunk."

I stopped typing into my cell phone and looked up, "Who? Are you sure he's on our flight?"

She shyly pointed towards an older white-haired man slumped over in a wheelchair parked against the far wall, "I think so?"

Instantly, I was happy to be working as the mid-cabin flight attendant. Not that I hated being the lead flight attendant, most of the time that's the position I work, but someday's — like this specific one — I didn't want to deal with all the bullshit. And by bullshit, I meant boarding the airplane. Which, I hate to say, is complete and utter bullshit. Boarding is a circus I wouldn't pay to attend. A spectacle I wouldn't let someone buy me a ticket to see. The only thing more chaotic than boarding an airplane is the Trump administration. My nostrils picked up the faint scent of drama floating towards the gate. I knew it was coming — I sensed it, and it was powerful. It overpowered the smell of freshly brewed coffee from the coffee shop, and it originated from our future wheelchair passenger parked against the wall.

I looked back down at my phone, "Well, you better talk to the gate agent because if he's drunk, he ain't coming on our flight." With that, I placed my cell phone in my front pocket, grabbed the handle of my luggage, and started my way down the jet bridge towards the airplane.

One of those moments I loved being the mid-cabin flight attendant.

On the airplane, I put away my luggage and started conducting my security checks. I immediately put the drunk passenger out of my mind, concluding that no passenger, visually intoxicated and slumped over in a wheelchair, would step foot on the airplane. A miniature pony would board the aircraft before Drunky McWheelchair.

As I confirmed the pressure gauge on two oxygen bottles stored in the overhead in, I stepped down from the front seat bank as Carla walked on the airplane. Brenda, the other flight attendant, was directly behind her.

Carla dropped her luggage onto the galley floor with attitude. Thud! "The gate agent supervisor is giving me a difficult time."

I closed the overhead bin and moved into the row allowing Brenda enough space to continue walking to the back of the airplane. "What do you mean she's giving you a hard time?"

Carla took a sip of her iced coffee and threw her purse onto the galley counter, "She's telling me the guy is not drunk. She said she talked to him and he's fine, but he's sitting there in the wheelchair arguing with himself."

With that, I knew I'd be getting involved. Carla's delivery of what occurred after I departed the gate triggered me like a snowflake. It's not one of my best traits. Not the fact that I'm an easily triggered snowflake, but that diving into drama on the airplane is a natural instinct. I initially come off as someone who doesn't want to deal with it, but the moment that shit pops up and out like a curious turtle's head — I'm ready to turn it into soup. There was no question now; I owned Drunky McWheelchair's drama as if I had initiated it myself. Had I? I had encouraged Carla to talk to the gate agent. Was it my fault we had problems before the first passenger stepped foot on the airplane? Was there another option? No. There wasn't. The only other option was ignoring the situation and not questioning whether the passenger was fit to fly.

That was out of the question. Flight attendants are there for the safety of all passengers, including the passengers left behind because they are too drunk to fly. Without another word, I stepped past Carla and walked into the flight deck. Luckily, we were flying with Captain Sue, a cool redhead based in LAX who takes zero shit from anyone. I expect that in her house — she wears the pants — and by pants, I mean strap-on dildo.

"Sue…"

She turned her head, "Joe! How the hell are ya? I haven't seen you in forever."

"I'm based in JFK now, but listen, we have what seems to be a drunk passenger in the gate area. He's sitting in a wheelchair talking to himself, and the gate agent says he's fine to fly. I don't —"

Not letting me finish, she leaped out of her jump seat and pressed past me, "No problemo. I got this. I'll be right back."

I stepped back into the galley as Carla finished her security checks. She took a sip of her drink, "What's happening?"

"That's Sue. She's fucking awesome. She'll talk to the gate agent and clear this shit up. Once we think someone might be drunk, we can't let them on the airplane. Not today."

She repeated, "Not today."

I raised it up a notch, "Not today... BITCHES!"

A few minutes later we began boarding. I positioned myself in the exit row ready to greet passengers while they found their seats. I stood there for only a few minutes until Captain Sue and Delilah, the gate agent supervisor, stepped onto the airplane. I could have stayed away and continued addressing passengers as they made their way to their seats, but I am too nosey for that shit.

I abandoned my post and squeezed between passengers and their bags, pushing my way to the front of the airplane. Once there, I planted myself in the front galley between Carla and Delilah. I stood with my arms folded trying to intimidate anyone who'd allow me.

Delilah was not happy. I expected she didn't appreciate the questioning by Captain Sue or the flight attendants. Either that or Sue got her right before she was about to go on her lunch break.

With her resting bitch face, she snapped, "I spoke to the passenger. He seems fine. Let's get him on the airplane and see how he does."

I looked at Sue and couldn't hold my tongue, "See how he does? That doesn't sound very convincing. You know we gotta fly with this guy, right?"

Then I turned to Delilah. She evaded eye contact and continued talking to Sue, "I think he may be disabled. We have to be careful when it comes to ADA laws."

Without skipping a beat, Sue responded, "Yes. I understand that. But if he was picked up by the wheelchair employee at the bar, and he's talking to himself at the gate, and it's obvious he's been drinking — then he must be drunk."

Delilah wasn't budging from her belief, "As I said, I spoke to him. He's probably on some medication."

Sue stepped back into the flight deck to talk with the first officer. Carla looked at me while passengers stepped onto the airplane and found their seats. I gave Delilah a look I give people when they refuse to put their pet in the carrier after I've asked them five times. It's a scary look. If I were Medusa, it would turn bitches to stone.

Let me talk to you about the Americans with Disabilities Act — the ADA — and how this act practically holds airlines by the balls. I promise you; it's not an exaggeration. I am pretty sure that if you walked into an airline CEO's office unannounced, they'd be standing beside their desk while a representative from the ADA had their balls cupped tightly in the palm of their hand. Not too tight. Not enough to prevent them from impregnating their second wife, just enough to let them know who's in charge.

JOE THOMAS

Women CEOs are not off the hook, either. I'd expect their ADA experience to be more like a mammogram.

First things first: I am not trying to start a war with the people behind the ADA. Second things second: I am not an enemy of the ADA, or of anyone who is disabled. That's almost impossible. I was a nurse for over a decade, and I promise you, I've assisted more disabled individuals than most people reading this book. The ADA is critical when it comes to preventing companies and employees from discriminating against someone with a mental or physical medical condition. But, if I am going to be completely honest, I do not agree with every single policy of the ADA regarding airline passengers. I expect many of you who are reading this will call me an asshole for what I am about to say, but I am staying true to my beliefs.

I support many policies that are in place; there's only one that I honestly disagree with, one that I roll my eyes at whenever it crosses my mind.

One of the most ridiculous and insane things the ADA ruling demands airlines do, which is choose wheelchairs over people.

I will repeat it, choose wheelchairs over people. And here you thought the airline treated you poorly by merely making you stand outside the gate in line like a bunch of cattle on death row. I am sure your initial question is, "Wheelchairs over people? What is this fuckery? I think Joe has finally lost it." I promise you; I've lost it, but not because of this. It's true, wheelchairs over people. The first time I heard this absurd policy, I thought I had slipped into an episode of *The Twilight Zone*. But instead of pig people, there were wheelchair people — and their wheelchairs had more rights than human beings.

94

Let me explain, as I can only imagine your heads are exploding all over the pages of this book. I hope it's not a library book, which will be a difficult stain to explain. Trust me, I know. In 1993, I sneezed on my copy of Madonna's book, *Sex*. It happened on a page where she was photographed doing a backflip in a pool. Not so bad except she was naked and her pussy was smack dab in the center of the page. Perfectly positioned next to her bush was my sneeze stain. Imagine spending decades trying to explain that it's a sneeze, and not my ejaculation shot.

Nobody seems to take my word for it when I share that story.

We all know airlines passengers can request wheelchair assistance when they arrive at the airport. Some passengers only require a wheelchair to get to the departing gate. Some just need it upon arrival at their final destination to assist them to baggage claim. It often depends on the size of the airport, or if the airport is in West Palm Beach. If you are flying out of West Palm Beach, Florida, you should know that nobody walks in that airport. Nobody. Toddlers request a wheelchair. The floors must be made of quicksand at that airport because everyone asks for a wheelchair. It's incredible. I once saw a Chihuahua in a wheelchair next to its human parent, who was also in a wheelchair. I guess the lady wanted her dog to feel her pain. I don't understand people from South Florida. Just know, that if you fly into Palm Beach International Airport, there will be a long wait while they board 20 passengers who requested wheelchairs.

Some require a wheelchair because they can only walk a few steps before falling as if an 8.7 seismic earthquake hit. Those are the passengers who need the wheelchair. It happened to me once; I needed a wheelchair when I had a gout attack while at Evan's house in Cleveland. The pain began in my knee, and I couldn't walk. I literally couldn't walk. To this day, I have never experienced that much pain. I'd take a step, shift my weight to the gout knee, and scream out in agony. My knee looked like Derek Jeter hit it and scored a home run. But often — and I know this from standing in the front of the airplane for years — most people request a wheelchair because they are lazy and don't want to wait in line.

Don't believe me? Just close your eyes and think back at that time you were standing in line at Disney's Space Mountain? Remember that? It was hot as fuck. You were miserable. You thought of nothing else but being back in your climate controlled hotel room napping on your bed. But no, your brats wanted to ride Space Mountain for the fifth time. Now, I want you to remember all those assholes who zipped past you in a wheelchair to the front of the line. Those young thirty-somethings with casts on their legs. If you have a cast on your leg, you shouldn't be cutting someone in line to get on Space Mountain; your ass should be at home watching Netflix.

I rest my case.

For some reason, and I don't understand, the ADA believes an assisted device, aka wheelchair, should take precedence over a human being.

Here's my example, Billy is a disabled guy who has a wheelchair. He calls the airline a few days before his flight and requests his wheelchair be stored inside the airplane for the trip. Not in the cargo hold, but INSIDE the aircraft. Yes, inside where we serve food and drinks to thirsty passengers. The airline complies with Billy's request because he has provided them with plenty of notice. The day of his flight, Billy arrives at the airport, and he is moved from his wheelchair to a different one at the gate. The gate agents bring his wheelchair onto the airplane to secure it. Some planes have personal lockers and storage bins for this exact circumstance. Some airplanes do not. Where I work, we do not have additional storage locations for a passenger's wheelchair. At my airline, we put the personal wheelchair in a row of seats. You heard that correctly, in a row of seats. What happens if it's a full flight? Do you want me to tell you, or can you guess? Fuck it; I'm going to share it with you. As shocking as it sounds, paid passengers get removed from the flight. That's not a lie.

Full disclosure, it's rare, but I have experienced how this affects other travelers. Many years ago, I was working a trip, and we had three open seats available on the flight. The scattered empty seats were throughout the airplane. A disabled passenger requested his wheelchair be secured inside the aircraft, so the gate agent resat passengers around, to leave the last row free for the wheelchair. That action resulted in three standby passengers not making their flight. Flight attendants unable to commute home after working because some selfish person requested their wheelchair travel like a human being.

As you can imagine, this topic burns my scalp like a day at the pool. I will repeat this, I don't have anything against disabled people, but I do have a problem with a wheelchair bumping any passengers off an airplane. I think it is fucking absurd. Another human being? Possibly. A wheelchair? No.

We're also not allowed to question or talk to the disabled passenger about it. That's the hardest part. Each time I walked by the passenger, I wanted to lean down and say, 'You know three people were left behind because of you. You know that, right?" But that's more of an ADA violation than tossing the wheelchair out of the airplane at 38,000 feet. Ask that question, and you may find yourself in a dumpster behind a rehabilitation clinic.

One day, because I push the envelope, I asked someone in a friendly voice why they would want their wheelchair secured on the airplane. The answer was, "Sometimes wheelchair get damaged in cargo."

I agree that must suck, but it's still not an excuse to leave behind paid passengers — or even standby passengers — to store a wheelchair in a row of seats. If I ever find myself wheelchair bound, I will never put my wheelchair before a real person. I'll never expect my wheelchair to fly like Lady Gaga in first class.

When you consider all this, it makes sense why gate agents are so frightened of an ADA violation. When I first started, I had no clue about the ADA. Sure, they gave us a rundown in flight attendant training, but I had more important things to focus on than worrying about the ADA. I was preoccupied with the other flight attendants clocking which pilots were open-minded to receiving fellatio while on layovers in boring cities. Cities like Milwaukee, where the only thing you can look forward to is a blowjob, or maybe a *Laverne & Shirley* marathon on Lifetime.

Seriously, I had no clue. If you were to stop me at the gate and ask me what the ADA stood for, I'd have guessed, The American Dick Association. It makes perfect sense if you're thinking about dick 23 1/2 hours a day. And I would have said it loud and proud because I am an American Dick Association card holder. I am an American, and I have a dick. When you think about it that way, a violation by the ADA sounds sexy.

But flight attendants don't worry about the ADA, or at least this one doesn't. I treat everyone with respect, care, and dignity. I've been treating people that way ever since my nursing days. I don't need the ADA to guide me on how to manage people. Sounds like Christians who need Jesus to stop them from kicking old ladies out of the way at Walmart. I do not need that; I don't even shop at Walmart. I have never once heard a flight attendant comment about fear for an ADA violation, but that's because they're always talking about being on disciplinary action for their horrible attendance.

Delilah refused to budge. Sue hadn't emerged from the flight deck, and Carla had finally finished sucking out the last bit of iced coffee from the bottom of the cup. It seemed like we reached a roadblock on how to move forward with this questionable passenger. The gate agent came running down the jet bridge and stepped onto the airplane. "We only have a few more passengers, what are we doing with the guy?"

Delilah answered, "We are boarding him. Bring him down."

With all her weight, Delilah broke through the road-block. I stepped out into the aisle by row one and addressed Carla, "Bring him on the airplane, and we'll see what happens." I began closing overhead bins in an aggressive manner — which meant I slammed them shut. An airline no-no, but sometimes you have to let your frustrations out on the airplane. It was either slam overhead bins, or slam Delilah on the top of her fat fucking head.

I went with the overhead bin.

I stopped at row five, turned around, and walked back up to the galley as the airport employee pulled the wheelchair up to the airplane door with Curtis in tow. As Curtis reached out, he grabbed the airplane door, and it became unlocked and started closing in on him. That's all we needed was him to injure himself before he stepped onto the airplane. It would have made sense though because this guy presented himself as being extremely intoxicated. He was so fucked up he could have been in *The Hangover*. But Curtis was so messed up; he didn't even make it in the movie. He overslept. I have been around enough drunk people to know an intoxicated person when I am looking down at them. Hell, I've been that drunk person.

I pushed the airplane door back into place, so it locked again, and put my hand out to Curtis, but he refused it. My feelings were not hurt. I'd have probably blown a 0.8 in the breathalyzer just from touching his skin. I moved out of the way as he stumbled onto the airplane.

My attitude quickly changed. My desire to leave Curtis behind at the airport to sober up was gone. I wanted him on the flight. I figured that if he passed out — or died — I'd be able to witness the termination of someone like Delilah. There'd be a lot of paperwork involved, but nothing I haven't had to deal with in the past. I turned to Delilah, "I can't believe you are allowing him on this airplane."

She snarled, "I can't believe you said that in front of the passenger."

I ignored her and moved closer to the lavatory and flight deck. I wasn't worried about Curtis, he was trashed and wouldn't hear us slamming into a 747 at the end of the runway — nevermind hearing me whisper something six feet away.

"Howdy," he said to each passenger as he gradually inched his way to row four. I watched him step over Mr. Jackson, the small man seated in the aisle, and then fall into 4F. I followed behind him while Delilah followed me carrying two of his small bags. One, a small tote bag that I took from her and placed above his row in the overhead bin, and two, a small brown paper bag from the airport store. She climbed into the window seat in row three, reached into the bag and pulled out his wallet handing it to him over the seat, "Curtis. You should hold onto this."

I rolled my eyes.

"No. You keep it," he answered in a dismissive tone.

She pushed the wallet towards him, "It's your wallet. You need to put it in your back pocket." Then she handed him the brown paper bag, which he grabbed and then dropped onto the floor. Delilah looked at me, and I smiled at her. She knew it wasn't a friendly smile.

Delilah crawled back over the seat bank and walked up to me, "He should be fine."

I responded, "Let's hope."

There was nothing else we needed to say to each other. My hands were tied. When the airplane is at the gate, the gate agent supervisor is in charge. The captain has the final say, but Sue had given up. She only came back out from the flight deck once to confirm our final decision. The agreement was to let Curtis board the airplane; there was no other information. Delilah walked up to the front galley and started talking to Carla. I stayed back to listen to Curtis as he reached into his jacket pocket, pulled out his cell phone, and made a call.

"Yeah. What? What? I can't hear you. Listen, this is Curtis. I'll be staying on the strip. Pick me up." I hovered around conversing with a few passengers while confirming his slurred speech. It was terrible, like being hammered but still trying to have a serious conversation with someone while acting sober. If you've ever been drunk, you know what I mean. It's when you're speaking slowly and over pronouncing each word, but it still all comes out like your teeth have come loose in your mouth, and you're trying to hold them all in.

The passengers in Curtis's row were all traveling together. Mr. Jackson, the senior citizen in the aisle seat on his side of the airplane, and three older women across the aisle seated in 4A, 4B, and 4C. I struck up a conversation, "So, you ladies heading to Vegas for some fun?"

The woman on the aisle frowned, "No honey, we going to a funeral. My cousin's Aunt Beatrice done passed away last week. We gonna help her and her family out."

That conversation ended quickly.

I moved down a few rows to make room for a family of four. They were the last four passengers to board the airplane. By this time, Curtis had ended his phone call and was now focused on the family shuffling down the aisle. His interest was in the two children following their parents.

He yelled out, "Come here, little girl. Sit next to me." Cringe-worthy to say the least. When he saw the boy, he added, "Come sit here skinny boy," patting the middle seat between him and Mr. Jackson. Curtis was a drunk and the president of the National Man-Boy Love Association. All in one day, and on my flight.

How did I get so lucky?

Once the little girl and skinny boy sat with their family in the middle of the airplane, I completed my exit row briefing and walked back to the front galley. As I passed Curtis, I noticed his head was down and his double chin rested on his chest. He was asleep. I hoped he stayed that way for the entire flight.

Delilah was still in the front galley eye fucking me as I walked up. Was she trying to intimidate me? That would only happen if she planned to lather me up with barbeque sauce and roast me on an open fire. She looked like a woman who could destroy an entire pig at a luau "Is he alright?"

I hated giving in, "He's asleep. Let's hope he stays that way."

"I think he's medicated," Delilah added as she walked towards the airplane door, "we have to be very careful with these types of situations."

Carla nodded. I turned away and began reading the manifest. The only medication Curtis had in his system was Jack Daniels on the rocks. Delilah closed the airplane door halfway, "Are we ready to close the door?"

"Yes. Ready to close the door."

Delilah pulled the door closed, the jet bridged moved away from the airplane, and we conducted our safety procedures. While I prepared for my safety demonstration, I looked over at Curtis, and he was wide awake chatting with the Mr. Jackson.

From that moment, Curtis never stopped talking. Happy to be the mid-cabin flight attendant, I went to the back of the aircraft the moment the airplane hit 10,000 feet. It was a short flight to Las Vegas, and we had no time to dilly dally. From Los Angeles to Las Vegas, we are lucky

103

to get 45 minutes to start and finish our beverage service. It might seem like a lot, but when you have a full flight, and people start ordering special requests, it can lead to chaos.

As the three of us zipped through the cabin like beverage fairies, my mind stayed busy with the passengers in my section. I had almost forgotten about Curtis until I walked up to the front galley to start a trash pick up through the cabin.

You could hear Curtis from the front galley, "I built this airplane. That's right. Took me a long time, but we got it done."

Carla was cleaning out a coffee pot as I walked into the galley, "Do you hear this shit? He's telling the guy next to him that he built this airplane."

She laughed, "Yeah. He asked for a whiskey, but I gave him water."

"Funny how that happens." I stepped into the aisle picking up cans; it didn't take me long to get to row four, where I overheard Curtis, "I own the love boat. Did you hear me? The love boat."

My eyes made contact with Mr. Jackson, who looked like he wished he was heading to his funeral instead of just being partially blind. If there was such a thing as ear cataracts, I'm sure he'd have wished he had them. I turned back around and walked the few rows back to Carla. "He just told the guy in 4D that he owns *The Love Boat*," I let out a loud laugh, "This guy is insane."

She didn't skip a beat as she took a sip of water, "Oh yeah. The guy seated behind him came up to use the lavatory and said he's talking about the love boat."

"I wonder if he's talking about the one from the TV show?"

"Do you know about another Love Boat?"

We both laughed.

Our 45-minute flight was over as quick as it started. In fact, we spent more time on the ground boarding than we did on our way to Las Vegas. The moment we arrived at the gate, I kept my eyes on Curtis. He had a wheelchair requested, but his behavior showed that he had no desire to use it. That did not surprise me. More passengers are touched by the Holy Spirit on an airplane than at a Pentecostal revival. When we boarded the flight in LA, he could barely walk onto the airplane, now in Las Vegas, he was practically doing somersaults down the aisle. He unbuckled his seat belt, fell on top of Mr. Jackson as he climbed out into the aisle, grabbed his carry on bag from the overhead bin, and stood in the aisle waiting to deplane. He swayed so much I almost got seasick. As Curtis strolled off the airplane, Carla asked him, "Sir, I thought you requested a wheelchair?"

He mumbled something, and then he was gone.

I began cleaning up the rows and seat back pockets as passengers deplaned. When I got to row four, I struck up a conversation with the Jackson family. No Janet, but I'd survive. "How many of you need wheelchair assistance?"

Three hands went up. That was the same number from this group who needed a wheelchair when we boarded. Funny how the Holy Spirit touched Curtis, but not Mr. Jackson. I guess it's better the Holy Spirit touched him instead of him molesting that skinny little boy.

"Perfect. Just remain seated until everyone deplanes and then we can help you without rushing you off the airplane."

Mrs. Jackson, I presumed, answered, "Oh yes sugar, we've done this a few times."

When the last passenger stepped off the airplane, I helped Mr. Jackson stand up and guided him towards Carla who was approaching row four from the front.

Mr. Jackson moved slowly. I took down a few of their bags when all of a sudden he turned around from row two and yelled, "Where's my bag? I can't find my bag."

I knew which bag he was referencing. It was a small blue bag that I initially tried placing in the overhead bin, but Mr. Jackson wanted it beside him because of his medications. Some people are like that with their drugs. If it's more than one inch away, it's too far. I guess that makes sense when you need a pill to survive and end up dropping dead because the overhead bin door got stuck.

"Where is it?" I asked as I helped Mrs. Jackson out of her seat. Carla had walked back to the front of the airplane making sure the extra wheelchairs were lined up at the door.

Mr. Jackson didn't seem as concerned as his wife. She spoke loudly, "It was right there," she pointed under the seat, "I bet you that loud white man took it. He's been trying to distract us the entire time just to take that bag."

I got on my knees and looked under the seats. No blue bag. I looked in the overhead bin — just in case — still, no blue bag. "I don't know what happened to it. I remember putting it right under the seat. We'll have to tell the gate agent."

When Mr. Jackson stepped into the front galley, his wife and I were two steps behind him. I looked out towards the wheelchair, and the first thing I saw was his blue bag in the wheelchair employee's hand. I announced, "There's your bag. The employee has it."

Carla stared at me as if I lost my mind as she took the last few steps with Mr. Jackson off the airplane.

Once all four of them were on their way to the terminal, I took a deep sigh. Sweat dripped down my forehead, so I stepped into the lavatory to dab myself with tissue. "Damn. That was fucking ridiculous. They stressed me out about that bag."

Carla sat in 1C for a moment, "What happened? I didn't know what you guys were talking about."

I wiped the sweat from my head and tossed the tissue into the trash bin, "The guy in 4D thought Curtis stole his bag because they couldn't find it. Had me on the floor searching for it."

Carla let out a laugh and started shaking her head. "That's funny. He handed me the bag when I walked down the aisle to meet him, and I gave it to the wheelchair guy. "

I flopped into 1D for the few minutes we had to decompress before we started boarding again, "These people are gonna give me a heart attack."

Looking at her phone, Carla added, "At least that crazy guy didn't die or cause too much of a scene."

"Yeah, that's good, and no harm came to any skinny boys or girls. That's good, too."

Murphy's Law.
More like, Joe's Law.

If swapping from a fantastic trip with a layover in Honolulu into one with a West Palm Beach (PBI) layover wasn't bad enough, I started out the day commuting to JFK in a middle seat. You might be asking, why did I swap into a horrible trip? I still question that decision. Some might say it was a lapse in judgment, others — including myself — will just call it what it was, mental illness.

At my seniority, I never have to step foot in Florida. I don't have to fly anywhere I don't want to. It's pretty fucking sweet. But sometimes shit happens, and we find ourselves swapping out of a great trip, that our seniority held, for a shitty one usually saved for reserve flight attendants.

I had been sick earlier in the week, so I switched to the West Palm Beach trip to give myself a few more days at home to recover. All I'm going to say is… it looked better on paper. Next time, I will call in sick.

Some flight attendants enjoy working flights to West Palm Beach. I've never met any, but there's a rumor they exist. I think it's all bullshit. Nobody with a functioning frontal lobe puts up with that type of abuse. I can't handle flights to West Palm Beach, and I usually refuse to put myself through that torture. I bet if given a choice, Jesus Christ would have stuck with the crucifixion over operating a flight to West Palm Beach.

Crew Scheduling: "Jesus… Jesus. Down here? Hey listen, we got this West Palm Beach turn we want you to work? It'll get you off that cross. Can we check you in for the trip?"

Jesus Christ: "What was that? I couldn't hear you."

C.S.: "WE HAVE A TRIP FOR YOU. A WEST PALM BEACH TURN."

J.C.: "Did you say West Palm Beach? Me on a cracker! Fuck that. I'm good right here."

Listen, Jesus endured nails hammered into his hands, so if he can handle that but not passengers on a West Palm Beach flight, I don't feel sorry.

Ft. Myers, Florida? Yes. Tampa? Yes. Orlando? Barely. West Palm Beach, Ft. Lauderdale or Miami? Fucking kill me. It all boils down to the selfish passengers. I've never experienced people so entitled and demanding in my entire life, and that's saying something — I work with pilots on a daily basis.

I'm not just a bitchy flight attendant. I am prepared to share examples. Here's one: during the flight to PBI, a male passenger yelled at me because he had to pay for a blanket. He shouted for a full minute, over a five dollar blanket. He never even tried bartering, just began tearing into me over the prospect of having to pull out his credit card. People may think, a full minute? That's not so bad. My wife yells at me for hours on end.

My advice for them: get a divorce lawyer.

It's not fun being yelled at for any length of time by a complete stranger over something you have no control over while standing in the middle of the airplane. When that happens, I use every cell in my body to fight my urge to shove the blanket down their throat.

That's a long fucking minute.

Then another male passenger was unable to log into the airplane's wifi connection. Even though I walked through each step with him carefully while I struggled to get my drink service done, this guy's electronic device refused to connect. Guess who's fault that was? Thankfully, I have broad shoulders and can handle carrying around drinks and manage a verbal reprimand because a passenger's electronic device sucks. Too bad it wasn't a Samsung Galaxy Note 7. I'd let him burn up before I reached for the extinguisher. During that entire interaction, I ended up helping five passengers log into the internet, so I guess I'm not that cruel and mean. Like everyone else, I love posting on social media at 38,000 feet; I just don't like people blaming me because they don't know how to work their phones. My husband works in the tech industry, not me.

One snippy lady said, "But your job is to log me into the internet."

I corrected her, "Actually, it's not. But follow the steps I gave you and good luck. We land in a few hours."

What I wanted to say was, "Bitch... Do I look like I work at the fucking Apple help desk? No!" My job isn't to make sure you stay connected to your family on Facebook during a two-hour flight. My duties are to bring you a drink, some nuts, and throw you into the raft if we land in the Atlantic Ocean. And that's the truth. The airline explicitly tells us that we can assist the passengers logging into the wifi, but we are not responsible for spending the entire flight attempting to connect them. Give them the directions on how to log in, and continue passing out beverages.

The same lady's cell phone battery was at 10%. Again, not my problem, but she had other ideas. "Do you have any plugs on this airplane?"

"I'm sorry, this airplane doesn't have outlets to charge devices."

"Do you have a portable charger that I can use?"

That was ballsy, "No. I'm sorry. I don't."

The guy sitting next to her interrupted, "They charge extra for that."

I shouldn't take things personally on the airplane, and I usually let things roll off my back, but we all have our breaking point. I shot daggers at him, "You know what? The wifi is free. So is the television. And the beverages. So, I'm gonna try and not be offended by your comment." Then I smiled my evil smile, the one that scares my husband and the cats.

"Don't be offended. I was just joking."

I ignored him. Like I said, rude people. If an asteroid slammed into West Palm Beach, nobody would care. Except the people living there and they'd be dead, so fuck it. It would just add more oceanfront property for everyone.

As we prepared to land at PBI, a woman came stumbling out of the lavatory. I was cleaning up the front galley and putting away cups. She asked, "Can I have a bottle of water? And two cans of orange juice?"

I reached for a cup, "Would you care for some ice?"

"No. I'm taking it for my drive home."

I handed her the items and shook my head while staring at her. She got the message. When the fuck did this airplane become a 7-Eleven?

The van ride to the hotel was tranquil. It was almost midnight, and the four of us (two pilots and two flight attendants) were exhausted. Not exhausted enough for the first officer to hit on the other flight attendant.

Amaya wasn't ugly, but she wasn't pretty either. At least that's my opinion. She reminded me of a sad drag queen who had auditioned for *RuPaul's Drag Race* six seasons in a row and continued getting rejected.

The first officer didn't seem to mind. I figured he must be a fan of the show. After collecting our room keys and piling into the elevator, he was on her like a bloodhound on a fox. "So, you gonna work out tomorrow morning?"

She never looked up from her phone, "Maybe."

"If you do, you should hit me up. I'd love a workout partner."

I tried not vomiting on my uniform shirt. I only carried one in my luggage.

"Yeah. That's cool." Amaya still hadn't looked up from her phone, "If we meet up down there then we can work out together."

"Here," he wasn't taking any chances, "let me give you my number."

I've never met a coworker so interested in another coworkers work out schedule. We had a short nine-hour layover scheduled, and this first officer wasn't fooling around. The only scheduling to be done was to find time to shower, sleep, and eat our complimentary breakfast. I doubted there would be any time for him to park his big black stallion in her tiny latin stable by the time the sun came up. But what do I know?

The next morning I rolled over in my hotel bed and said out loud, "Either today will kill me, or I'll be terminated." I can confirm that neither happened. I was preparing to fly — wait for it - West Palm Beach to Cleveland to Miami to Pittsburgh. Why not just fly to the fucking Moon?

After I finished a quick shower, I threw on my wrinkled uniform and headed downstairs to enjoy my complimentary breakfast. Using the word enjoy doesn't seem right when you have to scarf it down within five minutes so you can catch the hotel shuttle to the airport.

I wanted to eat breakfast in peace, but peace never comes to those who deserve it. A flight attendant from my airline pulled up a chair and sat down. I had never met her, and I had no desire to chat with anyone, but I quickly shared my true feelings. I tend to complain when I am tired after such a short layover. "If yesterday is any indication of how today is going to go, I may kill someone. I will literally stab someone."

"No, you won't. Can I ask you something? Are you Flight Attendant Joe?"

That always makes me feel better.

I finished my breakfast, grabbed a bagel for the road, and followed Amaya out of the hotel into the already humid Florida air. My mood was pleasantly shifting until we stepped onto the airplane and I found my galley an utter fucking disaster. The worst part was, I passed the flight attendants at the gate. Their pleasantries fooled me. When I find the galley looking like a hurricane made a direct hit, I want to run back up the jet bridge, through the airport, jump in front of the hotel shuttle van, yank them fuckers out, and drag them back to clean up the shit they left behind. Dirty coffee pots. Used coffee bags in the coffee machine. Beverage carts not swapped out. Finding the galley a mess before a flight is not uncommon. After almost ten years of this job, it still pisses me off. It's unacceptable that I — or anyone else — have to walk on an airplane and spend five minutes cleaning up after other flight attendants.

All you flight attendants in the world who are reading this: stop being so fucking lazy and clean up after yourself. If I wanted to do your job, I'd just work your flights.

The flight from West Palm Beach to Cleveland did not disappoint. When the gate agent brought me the boarding paperwork, she looked like she had run a marathon, "You have 12 wheelchairs. Can we board early?"

I laughed, "Twelve wheelchairs? We should have started boarding last night."

The first lady to board from one of the many wheel-chairs had a service animal. That's different than a pet or a comfort animal. When you travel with a pet, you pay a fee, and the pet stays in its carrier under the seat in front of you. When you travel with a comfort animal, you provide documentation that states you can fly with the pet in your lap because you can't handle functioning in the real world without your Pomeranian. Service animals have a job. They are working on the airplane like the flight attendants and pilots. They detect seizures. They help the blind. They don't do safety demonstrations and serve drinks though — that would be amazing. This dog was a service animal, and because of the size and demeanor of his boss, it was apparent he worked his little fucking ass off.

I am always friendly to service dogs as they walk onto the airplane. They usually look more confused than their employer. Maybe they want to commit suicide because slavery went out hundreds of years ago.

She said, — the lady, not the dog — "Mikey yelps a lot. I hope he doesn't disturb everyone." Something told me that would be inevitable. I smiled until she found her seat and they disappeared into the row.

Here's the thing about service pets: they shouldn't yelp a lot. Once boarded and in their assigned seat, I shouldn't have even known Mikey was there unless something happened to trigger him to do the job he was trained to do. Remember, they are technically working. You don't see me yelping throughout the flight, do you? Well, you might if someone demands that I log them into the wifi. When a passenger warns me about their service dog, I immediately question the legitimacy of their service dog status. But our hands are tied. If the passenger brought the appropriate documentation and showed it to the gate agent, there's nothing we can do.

After takeoff, I did a full reset of the in-flight televisions because half the airplane was lit up with flickering white screens. It's usually a simple fix. It's not like we lost an engine over the Pacific, or ran out of Dr. Pepper on a Dallas flight. It's a fucking television. I made my friendly announcement informing the passengers of the situation, but it seemed not everyone was listening.

4B wasn't happy, "Excuse me, how long will the television be out?"

I smiled, "Only for about five minutes. I had to do a full reset because there were many televisions not working.

115

She snapped, "I didn't pay to fly on an airplane with no television. I paid to watch TV on this flight."

My smile disappeared, "And you will, once they come back on." I walked away.

A few minutes later, she waved her hands to catch my attention in the galley. When I walked over, she asked, "Why is it so cold on this airplane?"

I smiled again, "Are you cold?"

"I wouldn't have said it if I wasn't."

My smile disappeared, again. This lady wanted to get slapped. Lucky for her, I wanted my next paycheck. "I will contact the flight deck to see if we can make it more comfortable for you. Have you shut off your air vent?"

"What? My air what?"

I reached above her head, "Oh yeah. It's on full blast. Let's turn this off, so the air isn't blowing directly on you."

She scowled, "Don't do that. I want fresh air. I just want you to make the airplane warmer. And you skipped over us. I need a spicy tomato juice."

"You had your eyes closed when I took drink orders; I didn't skip over you. I'll be right back with your juice." I calmly — and I say that loosely — walked to the front galley, opened up the cart, grabbed her juice, a cup of ice, and I may have slammed the cart shut. I mumbled a few profanities, but I couldn't begin to remember them all if I tried.

I walked the few steps to her row and placed her request on the tray table, "Here's your juice." I began to turn around and walk away when her hand went straight back up in the air. If she made it off the airplane without me snapping her arm in half, it would be a baby Jesus miracle.

116

"I said spicy tomato. This isn't spicy tomato."

I gaily spun around. When a gay guy gaily spins around, prepare yourself, because it's probably not going to be pretty. Prettier than her hacked up hairdo, but not pretty like me after eight hours of undisturbed sleep. Her husband took a break from staring out of the window, looked over at me, and then went back to looking out the window.

"It's not?" I reached for it and took it from her hand. I knew it was a can of spicy tomato juice because I can read and because I work on the airplane. But I wanted to entertain myself with this lady for a moment. I turned the can over in my hand and then emphatically stated "No. You're wrong. It's spicy tomato. See." I positioned the can two inches from her head and let her read the words.

She grabbed the can and cracked it open. I looked at her husband and said, "Sir, would you care for something to drink?"

He refused to make eye contact. He leaned into his wife's ear, whispered something, and then she looked up at me, "He'd like a Sprite Zero."

I didn't have the energy even to question why he didn't directly speak to me.

I continued conducting my beverage service. I wasted so much time with this unpleasant lady and her mute husband that half the passengers in my section still had not received their drinks. With a tray full of beverages, I approached row seven and was about to hand over a cup of hot tea when the white-haired lady in 7D tossed her rolled up newspaper onto my tray.

Oh, West Palm Beach, why don't you just fall into the ocean?

All the cups started toppling over, so with my cat-like reflexes, I batted the newspaper back off the tray and into her lap. She must have been reading some terrible news if she couldn't wait a few seconds until I had cleared off my tray. She was old, but I don't believe she was blind. I'm 99% sure that she was not reading *USA Today* in braille. Also, the gate agent never informed me about a blind passenger in 7D who liked throwing shit at you during the flight.

All I will say is, I hoped she wasn't wearing Depends.

We landed in Cleveland, and our Miami flight was departing from a different airplane. That's never fun. Flight attendants and pilots rarely stay with the same aircraft all day, especially when we have multiple flights to work. When we do keep the same airplane, it's a pay bonus. It takes time to unload your luggage off one plane, run through the airport, board another one, redo all the security checks, and then smile as passengers board. If time is money, keeping the same airplane is cash.

Lucky for Amaya and I, our new departure gate was only a few down from where we landed. I am a stickler for being on time. I probably get this from when I was a nurse, and it was drilled into our heads to always be on time with passing medications. In the nursing world, that is important. You have people's lives in your hand, on the airplane you just have to depart on time. But to the airline, they act like people will die if the flight attendants arrive at the gate late. That's not an exaggeration.

While sidestepping past passengers in the gate area, and dragging my bags from one gate to the next, I turned to see Amaya staring at her cell phone and strolling behind me without a care in the world.

I waited at the gate until she caught up, "We have to get on the airplane. We're scheduled to board in like five minutes."

"That's no my problem. We land late." Her accent destroyed the English language, but not in a cute and hot Sofia Vergara way — more like nails on a chalkboard Tattoo from *Fantasy Island* way.

"Yes. But we still need to get the flight out on time." I grabbed the paperwork, showed my ID to the gate agent, and walked down the jet bridge.

The gate agent yelled out, "The third flight attendant is already on board."

This was a split pairing, something my airline started in hopes to improve our on-time departures. Shockingly, it made it worse. At least if not worse, no better. I've never understood the logic of the split pairing, so it must be above my pay grade. A split pairing is when, at any time during the scheduled trip, you can work on a different airplane type (different than the one you initially started on) requiring additional flight attendants. On the first day, Amaya and I worked together on a smaller airplane. On day two, we operated a larger plane — with a third flight attendant. On the third day, Amaya and I were back flying on a smaller airplane.

Our third was Blaine.

Blaine and I have a history together. Not too dramatic, but one that I should share.

A few years ago, while based in Cleveland, I worked with Blaine. We were flying across the country with Bill. Bill was kinda different. He was obsessed with another airline. When I say obsessed, I mean Glenn Close *Fatal Attraction* obsessed. If he had a chance to leave a boiled bunny on the doorstep of their headquarters — he probably would.

We were mid-flight and Blaine was cemented to his jumpseat with a book glued to his hand. I am all for reading an all-embracing book on the jumpseat, but you should never ignore your duties as a flight attendant. And that's what Blaine did while Bill pranced back and forth from the front of the airplane to the back galley.

After the third time, I asked, "Bill, do you need some help up there? What's going on?"

He smiled, "It's just row 14. They keep ordering drinks," he looked over at Blaine, "I'm bringing another set of drinks to 14C. Can you charge them?"

Without looking up from his book he pushed over a piece of paper, "Write it down for me."

I lost my mind. Honestly, I forgot I was working on an airplane. I am not proud of that moment, but it happened. I lashed out, "Why are you sitting there while Bill's doing all your work? Get up and take care of your section."

Blaine slowly look up from his book, "Excuse me? He didn't ask."

"He doesn't have to ask. It's your section. Answer your call lights and put your book down. You haven't even done any trash throughout this entire flight. Get up and do something."

Bill froze in place while standing against the galley wall. He finally squeaked out, "It's okay. Just charge them."

"You know, Joe, you don't have to be such a bitch about it. You could simply ask me to help." Blaine responded standing up allowing his jumpseat to slam into place.

I felt bad. Blaine was right. There were ten other ways to handle that situation, and I went straight to the eleventh. My outburst worked though because Blaine put his book down and went through the airplane collecting trash. Not only that, he charged row 14 for all the drinks that Bill brought to them. When he walked back into the galley, it was chilly — and not because of the temperature.

Sheepishly I said, "I'm sorry. I didn't mean to attack you. I was just pissed that you were sitting there while Bill was doing all the work."

Blaine smiled, "It's okay. You were right. I was so into my book, and I should have gotten up. But damn, no need to attack me like that."

I laughed, "I know. I'm a bitch."

"You need some dick. That's what you need. The way you just yelled at me tells me you need to get fucked."

The truth always hurts, but it was nice that we were able to resolve our conflict so quickly. It would be fantastic if Twitter arguments were solved so peacefully.

I hadn't flown with Blaine since then, but here I was back in Cleveland flying with him and Amaya. When Amaya and I walked on the airplane, Blaine was seated in 1D waiting for us.

"Took you long enough. I already did all the security checks."

"Thank you," I leaned down to hug him and stepped out of the way for Amaya to make her way to the back of the airplane. Before she got past row five, the captain stopped us all to conduct the crew briefing. As he finished speaking, the gate agent stood at the door. I figured she was about to ask us if we were ready to board, but instead, a non-revenue passenger stepped onto the airplane and stared at me in the front galley. Things were chaotic while the pilots pulled their luggage inside the flight deck and provisioning stood behind me with the other airplane door opened swapping out beverage carts. There wasn't much time to think about why this passenger was standing in front of me before I had agreed to board. Typically, we allow non-revenue flight attendants and pilots to board before other passengers — as long as they have a seat — but the gate agents usually ask us before they walked them down the jet bridge.

I had no time to think about all that, "Welcome. Are you a flight attendant?" I didn't let her answer, "go ahead and take your seat. We're gonna start boarding shortly."

"I'm not a passenger. My name is Samantha; I'm here to do your safety checkride."

Time stood still. In Madonna's song, "Hung Up," she sings about time going slowly, but at this moment, it fucking stopped.

Samantha was there to do my checkride. Why not? The day I operated three flights up and down the east coast with Amaya, who looked like Chi Chi Rodriguez from *Too Wong Foo, Thanks For Everything, Julie Newmar*. Why not just push me out of the airplane door to the ground below to see if I survive? It would be less painful than dealing with all this bullshit in one day. I stared at her for what seemed to be a month and then smiled, "That's great. Just have a seat, and I'll be with you after service." I ushered her into her seat and tried forgetting she was there once we started boarding.

This was undoubtedly a Murphy's Law moment, if something can go wrong, it will. But in this case, it was more Joe's Law, if something can go wrong and fuck up Joe's day, it will.

Here's the thing, I don't usually worry about check-rides. I also don't worry about authority at my airline. Some flight attendants are petrified of management. I imagine they lay in bed expecting their supervisor to leap out of the closet and write them up for sleeping past their alarm clock on their day off. I do my job to the best of my ability, and if I end up getting terminated one day, then so be it. I have enough things intimidating me: skinny queens at a pool party, skinny queens at the bar, skinny queens in the crew lounge; the list goes on and on. I refuse to allow management to do that, especially at my airline, because most of them are skinny queens.

During boarding, Amaya pissed me off. Blaine wasn't helping my temperament, either. While I greeted passengers, I noticed that Amaya was not in the aisle helping passengers. That's a requirement for my airline. You don't have to lift bags all by yourself, but you are required to assist passengers with lifting their bags, helping them find their seats, closing overhead bins when they are full, and anything else needed. That's why it's the cabin bitch position. We've all worked it. Some of us like it, some of us don't.

I looked down the aisle and could see Amaya and Blaine chatting in the back galley. I picked up the interphone and called to the back. Blaine answered, "This is Blaine."

"Hey, can you have Amaya go stand in the aisle? I'm having a checkride done, and I don't want to get dinged for something someone else isn't doing."

"Okay."

A few moments later, Amaya and her caked on makeup were in the aisle. To be honest, I didn't care if she was helping people or planning workouts with passengers at our crew hotel, I just wanted her in place for when Samantha started checking off boxes.

It wasn't until after our safety demonstration, that I realized Blaine and Amaya would not be team players during my checkride. It's an FAA requirement that flight attendants take their seats immediately after the safety demonstration and compliance check. The only exception is in an emergency situation, and if that happens, we are going back to the gate anyway. It makes sense. The airplane is taxiing to the end of the runway to depart, and the pilots don't have time to wait for us to take our sweet ass time sitting down when they are ready to take off.

Taking the jumpseat immediately is difficult for some flight attendants. Did I say some? I meant most. Not for me. I hate to sound like one of those people, but I always take my jumpseat right away. It doesn't matter if I am the back galley flight attendant or the lead flight attendant. I also try not micromanaging. Harping on flight attendants to take their seats after the safety demonstration takes too much energy. That's energy needed for demanding passengers. We hire adults to be flight attendants, not children, and I am no parent. If the pilot watches them in the camera and reports them for sitting down at the last possible minute — not my problem.

This flight was different; it was a checkride. One of the things Samantha was looking for was if I could control the airplane environment, and that includes the flight attendants.

I secured my galley, shut off the lights, and took my seat. I sat there for a few minutes when I realized that Amaya was not walking down the aisle towards the front galley.

Why do people always put you in a fucking uncomfortable situation? I called to the back galley, and Blaine answered the interphone, "Blaine, can you have Amaya come take her jump seat, please?"

He snapped, "Honey. You're out of control."

I hung up. I may have been out of control, but I like shit done correctly, but that's difficult when you have incompetent flight attendants.

When Amaya got to her jumpseat, she pushed back a little, "I no understand why I sit down? I no get my checkride."

This bitch. "Samantha can do a surprise checkride on you if she notices that you aren't doing your job. Just follow the rules, and you will be fine."

"She can? I no think so."

I laughed, "I do. Now buckle up and please don't take your cell phone out while we are on the jumpseat.

Service went by quickly as I continued making eye contact with Samantha. She'd smile. I'd grin and think, Bitch. Why are you here today? Any day but today. Tomorrow? Next Friday? At that point, the only problem I had encountered was a small female passenger who had her feet on the tray table across the row from Samantha. Would she mark me down if I said something? If I didn't say anything?

I didn't give a fuck. I marched up to the passenger, and her dirty bare feet, and bent down within earshot of

Samantha, "Hi. Can you please take your feet off the tray table?"

She looked at me, "Why?"

Does the flight attendant have to explain why you should take your feet off the tray table? They do. "Because people eat on that tray table. Please take them down."

She huffed and took her feet down. I looked over at Samantha, and she whispered, "Thank you." At least I did something right.

The pilots came out for a lavatory break, and I sent Amaya into the flight deck while I stood guard in the front galley. Amaya left me with no confidence that she'd follow the procedure for lavatory breaks.

When the flight deck was secured, I sent Amaya through the airplane to collect trash, and I walked up to Samantha, "I'm ready for you."

She jumped up and followed me to the front galley.

"How are you today?"

"This is the worse day for a checkride, but I'm ready."

She laughed, "I'm sorry. There's nothing to be scared about."

I laughed right back, "Oh, I'm not scared. I'm well aware of this entire process. I just want to make sure the other flight attendants are doing what they are supposed to be doing."

"Agreed. Okay. I'd like you to show me exactly how you complete your security checks."

"Do you want me to pull equipment out?"

"No. Just tell me what you are doing."

That made sense. No need pulling out emergency equipment and giving the little old Miami ladies a heart attack in the front row. Although if they did have a heart attack, I'd have the AED in hand.

"Okay. Well, I start over here by the jumpseat…" and I proceeded to point out each piece of equipment I reviewed, what I checked for, and quickly moved onto the next item. As I went through the emergency equipment, Samantha marked off things on a sheet of paper. It's an odd feeling getting a checkride. You do security checks each time you walk on the airplane, but when you have someone watching you like you're stealing minis out of the liquor cart, it's an uneasy feeling.

When I concluded, I put my hands on my hips and looked around the galley one last time to make sure I was confident in what I had expressed. Feeling confident I said, "That's it."

She looked up from her clipboard, "Are you sure?"

Am I sure? Would I have said 'that's it' if I was unsure?

I gave another sweep with my eyes. Jumpseat area? Check. Lavatory? Check. Galley? Check. "No. I'm sure."

"You forgot to tell me that you close the latches over the galley carts?"

"Really?" I sounded snippy, "That's a given."

"Not exactly. You have to tell me you are doing that."

"Oh."

"And you forgot to tell me that you push open the lid of the lavatory garbage shoot and look inside there."

"Yeah," I disliked repeating myself, "That's a given, too. That's just common sense."

"I know it's nitpicky, but if you don't tell me those things I have to mark it off as you missed it."

Now, here's the kicker about these checkrides: we don't get in any trouble if we screw things up. I guess there's the off chance that someone could be so horrible that they are pulled off the flight and sent back to remedial flight attendant training, but I believe that's rare. I've never heard of it happening.

Samantha laid out her paperwork on my front galley, "You did a fantastic job. You just missed those two things about the lavatory trash lid and the cart locks."

I disagreed with her about that. I didn't miss them; I just forget to verbalize it. I kept that to myself. The faster she was back in her seat, the better I'd be. As she continued hammering on the pilots turned on the seat belt sign.

Listening to Samantha, I walked over to the inter-phone, put my finger up to pause her talking for a moment, and then made my PA, "Ladies and gentlemen, the captain has turned on the seat belt sign. Please return to your seats and fasten your seat belts." I hung up the interphone, "I'll be right back."

I walked down the aisle reminding passengers to follow my instructions. I glanced at the back galley waiting for Blaine or Amaya to step out and start a compliance check in their sections, but I'd be waiting a long time. The rule is only one flight attendant has to do a compliance check throughout the entire airplane when the seatbelt sign illuminates. I stopped at the end of my section and walked back up to Samantha to finish my checkride.

"Do you think they're gonna come out of the galley and do a compliance check?"

I folded my arms, "I have no idea. I doubt it at this point."

"You know, as the lead flight attendant, it's your responsibility, if they don't come out, to do the full compliance check. At least one of you has to go out there."

"I get it," I stood there against the galley counter, "I just wanted to see if they would come out and help me out. I'm not happy with those two right now."

"Would you like me to address it with them?"

"No. I'll go back there when we finish."

She frowned, "Alright. I'm sorry you have to work with people like this today, but now I have to mark that there wasn't a full cabin compliance check done when the seatbelt sign came on."

"That's fine. Excuse me while I go to the back and talk to my flight attendants."

Their lackadaisical behavior set my emotions on fire as if I had drunk tabasco for lunch. I stormed to the back galley the moment Samantha took her seat.

Blaine was seated on his jumpseat reading a book; that was not a surprise. Amaya was counting the phone numbers she picked up during drink service. That or she was viewing something on her phone. Who the fuck knows? Who the fuck cares? "Why didn't one of you come out and do a compliance check when the seatbelt sign came on?"

Stares. No words. Just stares. Then Blaine went back to his book. Amaya spoke up, "I no think we have to if you are there."

"Yeah. That's true, but you could have helped me out. You know I'm getting a checkride."

Blaine spoke up, "Sorry, Joe. I didn't think about it."

Amaya jumped in again, "We have to do that every time the light comes on?"

I could barely look at Amaya without wanting to strangle her with oxygen tubing.

When we landed in Miami, we said goodbye to Blaine and picked up a different flight attendant. I wasn't sad to lose Blaine; I'm just glad we made it through the day without me yelling at him and him calling me a bitch. Our new flight attendant was a young, attractive, muscular, black guy who made Amaya forget how to act at the gate, which wasn't great because we had a two-hour delay. The way she gushed over him, I expected to follow her around with a mop for the rest of the night. Lucky for me, I think she had on absorbent panties.

I stepped up to the podium to check the flight manifest. We were flying Miami to Pittsburgh, and I was hoping it was a light load. It wasn't. We were full.

"Can we kick off a few people? Like 100?"

The pimply faced gate agent laughed, "No. Then I'll be stuck with them. I'm not having that tonight."

Acne and attitude. A combination I was not ready to deal with, especially when I was dealing with the Latin Aphrodite collecting phone numbers like the Grim Reaper collects souls. When I stepped back over to Amaya and Jerome, she was already taking down his phone number. I couldn't make sense of it. As I said, she wasn't ugly, but she wore enough makeup for the entire cast of *Cats*. What she did have were big tits, and what I've learned from my straight friends is — big tits trump everything. Ugly face? Nope. Ugly face with big tits? Maybe. Especially with enough alcohol. But we were as sober as the leader of an AA meeting. I shook my head and sat as far away from them as possible until the airplane landed.

The flight to Pittsburgh was forgettable except for the passenger who walked onto the airplane and yelled, "This delay is Obama's fault."

I ignored him as he found his seat. I was disappointed when I realized he was in my section. During beverage service, he asked, "What beers do you have?"

After I recited them, he asked, "How do the beers come?"

I repeated. "How do the beers come?"

"Yeah man, how do they come?"

"They come in a can."

"Alright. I'll have a Bud Light."

I had never wanted to be in Pittsburgh, or at a hotel, so quickly in my entire life. I'd have been happier at a Donald Trump rally than flying at 38,000 feet.

The next day, Amaya and I were back working together on the smaller airplane. At least I didn't have to worry about her spending time collecting numbers from other flight attendants instead of doing her job. We waited in the hotel lobby for the van driver; he was supposed to pick us up at 4:00 p.m., but it was 4:10 p.m. when he finally pulled up into the porte-cochère.

He put our bags in the back of the van, and we climbed inside. As he closed his door, he announced, "I have to swing by and pick someone else up."

I looked at him from the back of the van, "We don't have much time. We're already leaving late. Do you know how long this is going to take?"

"When do you have to be at the airport?"

"We have to be at the gate by 4:25."

He pulled out of the hotel parking lot, "You should make it."

What did he mean we should make it? What kind of bullshit was that? All I thought was, we better fucking make it. I looked from the driver to Amaya and then realized —

if we spun out of control and hit a tree, the only person who'd be injured was Amaya because she wasn't wearing her seat belt.

The van driver advanced into an industrial park at top speed and stopped instantly. He had no clue where to pick up this other passenger. I was livid. He drove around the parking lot two times, and then pulled the van over and called the hotel, "Where's this passenger I'm picking up?"

At this point, my blood pressure medication was failing. My heart thumped around in my chest like a trout on a dock. After the driver received the answer he was looking for from the hotel employee, he put the van in drive, and we all flew backward. He pulled into a different parking lot across the street and parked in front of a glass building. Without a word, he stepped outside and stood against the van looking around.

"What the fuck is this dude doing? We gotta go." At this point, I didn't care if he heard me. I hope he did because I was furious. Amaya barely spoke; she was too busy on her cell phone. After standing outside the van for a brief moment, he ran into the building through the double glass doors. I peered out the van windows and around the parking lot like I was waiting for a sniper to start shooting.

Another minute or so passed before he finally emerged from the building with a fat man trailing him. He opened the back door, threw fatties bags in, and they both climbed into the van and closed their doors. Who was this guy? Was he important? Like the Mayor of Pittsburgh, or better yet, the owner of Primanti Brothers? The latter made sense. With the size of his belly, he looked like the type of guy who'd create a sandwich topped with french fries.

The Dickhead Van Driver (that's his official name) dropped us off on the other side of the airport. Not where he was supposed to drop us off — NO — but further away to face unnecessary obstacles as we tried getting to the gate. I am not against walking — I love to walk — but not when walking turns into running because I am late and being forced to go through TSA security because there's no Known Crewmember access where he dumped us off. That was the last straw for me; I did not tip him after he pulled my bags out of the back of the van. I hope that dollar I withheld was the difference between him ordering a Quarter Pounder with cheese for dinner or a cheeseburger. I avoided him as I yelled for Amaya to hurry so we could get to the gate without being reported to crew scheduling.

We had one short flight to work and then the trip would be over. A quick Pittsburgh-to-Boston flight, and then a deadhead to Cleveland. Before boarding, I called Amaya to review service standards. She immediately started arguing regarding serving coffee. I think she was arguing. Honestly, I don't know. Like I said before, she fucked up the English language. It was easier to understand a drunk Irishman. I politely reminder Amaya that we served coffee on the flight. Listen, I hate serving coffee. Hate it!! I hate it so much, that last sentence received two exclamations. I am a firm believer airlines should halt serving coffee immediately. We are in a metal tube, flying around pockets of angry, turbulent air, and managing hot liquids. Who thought that shit was a good idea? It's a hazard. But, I am paid to serve coffee, so I serve it. And if that was a problem for Amaya, well that was too damn bad.

When we landed in Boston, the captain and I stood in the front galley thanking passengers for flying with us. A young woman walked up the aisle, stopped at row one, and scooted into the row. She looked at me and then at the captain; she spoke evenly, "I want to complain about that flight attendant in the back. I asked her what beverages were available and she refused to tell me. She said, 'Look at the menu card,' and walked off. And then came back and said, 'Have you decided?'. I've never been so insulted."

The captain and I stumbled over our words. I finally spoke, "I'm so sorry about that. Is there anything I can do for you?"

She flung her bag over her shoulder, "No. I don't have an issue with you; it's her. She has a nasty attitude."

The captain looked over waiting for me to say something else. I didn't. He added. "I encourage you to write a letter to the airline. I will also talk with her."

She stepped back into the aisle, "Thank you. I will write a letter. I just, I mean... I can't believe how nasty she was. If you don't like doing this job, you should quit."

With that, she walked off the airplane. I grabbed my bags, and noticed the captain was standing in the galley. He was ready to confront Amaya, and I refused to miss it. My flight to Cleveland was delayed which gave me plenty of time to watch the show.

She strolled up the aisle looking at her phone. The captain pounced, "A passenger just complained that you were rude to her regarding beverage service."

Amaya took a moment to finish her text — this bitch's balls were enormous, bigger than anything I had ever seen — and responded, "No. She was rude. She no understands to look in the menu. It's no my job to tell her what we have."

The captain was beside himself. He glanced my way, but I had nothing to offer up. If I had a bag of popcorn, I'd have planted myself in row one.

"It's your job. That's literally your job."

She stared at him. I expected she was considering pulling the language barrier card, but she stood by her convictions.

"No. My job is to help in an emergency, not to stand and wait for a passenger to order."

He grabbed his luggage, "I encouraged that passenger to write a letter to the airline about you. Be on the lookout for that."

Amaya walked off the airplane without turning back. The captain looked at me as we left the aircraft together, "Can you believe that behavior?"

"Yes. I can. I'm just glad she didn't get your phone number."

He stopped, "What do you mean?"

I laughed, "It's a long story," I continued up the jet bridge, "Nice flying with you. I gotta catch my flight."

Journal Entry:
God's Waiting Room

Dear Journal,

Driving north on the 405 from San Diego to Los Angeles would test Buddha's patience if he was still alive. Instead of flying home to San Francisco for one day, I rented a car and drove down to San Diego to visit Justin for the night.

But before I go any further, let me share my experience at the rental car counter. The agent was gay and started hardcore flirting after I walked up to the counter. I don't remember his name, but he mentioned something about topping and giving me what I wanted. I can't recall his exact words, but all I wanted was a free upgrade, not an STD from a stranger. Honestly, he looked like he takes Retrovir daily if you know what I mean. I'm being serious; he had more lesions on his arms than a burn victim.

Anyway, he handed me the wrong paperwork and keys; I didn't realize it until I tried getting into the car. I equate that to riding the hotel elevator 19 floors, walking down a long hallway, trying to enter the room, and the key not working.

I hate that even more.

I walked back to the counter and stood to the side waiting to catch the eye of a different homosexual agent because my guy was not at his post. Probably AZT time. It took the agent a few seconds to make eye contact with me, and when he did, I politely said, "The other guy gave me someone else's paperwork."

He rolled his eyes confirming that these two queens were not best friends.

While I patiently waited for my paperwork, a heavyset (alright, the chick was fat as fuck), Latina woman walked past me and flopped her ham hock arm across the counter. Without looking over at me (I was about three inches from the hock part of the ham), she started in about her car not being something blah blah blah…

My anger fogged the sound coming from her lips smacking together.

I yelled out for everyone to here, especially her, "Excuse me? Do you know you just walked right past me? I have a problem too."

She looked at me. The queen behind the counter looked at me. I think he whispered, "Run," but I was too pissed off to comply.

She grabbed her keys, stepped aside, and started texting. Probably texting her Mexican mafia brother's cousin's father's uncle's best friend to meet me outside the airport to show me what happens behind the scenes at an El Chapo barbeque.

One day this no-filter brain will get me killed. The agent handed me the correct keys and avoiding eye contact with anyone; I hightailed it out of there before her 20 brothers showed up and jammed the rental keys up my ass.

It was a quick visit to see Justin, but well worth the time behind the wheel. When I visit Justin, it's like a mental health day. That's the best way to describe it. We caught up, had dinner, a few drinks, and I did laundry to prepare for my red-eye flight to Ft. Lauderdale the following night.

When it was time to leave his house, I gave myself four hours to get back to LA, which was plenty of time. After stopping for gas, I arrived at the airport and turned in the rental by 5:15 p.m. and still had 45 minutes to change into my uniform and release some of the stress the 405 poured all over me like hot coffee.

I had never worked with these two flight attendants, so it was a mystery of what I'd be getting myself into with this pair. Sometimes reporting for duty is like participating in an office secret Santa, you never know what you are going to get, or whether you are going to like it.

I did know one of the flight attendants though, and he's into puppy play. Not like running in the park with his dog, but barking while wearing a butt plug attached to a tail. I wonder what kind of Scooby snacks are in his pantry. I had so many questions for him that I expected the flight to be like a special on *20/20*.

His answers were what I had expected and more.

While I was in the flight attendant lounge, printing pairings for the three of us (I was the lead flight attendant), the other flight attendant working with us walked into the room, whispered something to Pound Puppy, and quickly walked out. She neglected to say hello, or goodbye.

I hate to admit this, but I chased after her, "Hello? Where are you going? We have to brief."

She looked at me funny, like, how dare I talk to her like that, "I told the other guy I'd meet him at the gate."

Am I invisible? I'm slightly chubby, so I know she saw me sitting at the printer, "Well, we need to brief and I'm the lead flight attendant, so I need to know what's going on."

It sounds much worse in print than it did when I said it in person. I promise.

Our flights for the night were Los Angeles to Las Vegas and then a red eye to Ft. Lauderdale. And because it's Daylight Savings Time, we will lose an additional hour as we travel across the country. Why do we even do that? DSL? Are we rising at 5:00 a.m. to milk cows? Does 85% of the population still live on farms?

The pilots walked on the airplane, and the first officer demanded, "I need three orange juices and four bottles of water, please."

The captain responded before I did, "Damn. It's only a 45-minute flight."

I laughed while opening the cart and handing him his order like I worked at the Kum & Go.

Once we landed in Las Vegas, we had about an hour to wait until our next flight. To stretch my feet, and enjoy the hum of the airport slot machines, I brought Pound Puppy for a walk through the terminal. I'd like to report that he did not pee on the carpet as we watched the British Airways flight pull away from the gate bound for Gatwick Airport.

After departure, I hung out for most of the flight in the front galley. I occasionally made my way to the back to check on Pound Puppy and the other flight attendant, but other than that, I spent most of my time writing in the front galley.

Because it's DST at 2 a.m., I answered numerous questions from senior citizens on the flight. The main question being, what time will it be in Ft. Lauderdale when we land? And because they're all deaf, I had to answer that question over and over again. It didn't matter that I had mentioned to the passenger in 4A we were landing at 6:00 a.m., the moment I walked away, 4B rang the call bell and asked, "What time will it be when we land?"

Fuck, it confuses me, and I'm wearing a watch and understand how time zones work. I'm pretty sure most of these passengers were born before the creation of time zones. It's like *Cocoon* at 38,000 feet. Man do I wish Steve Guttenberg had been a passenger. Steve Guttenberg from *Police Academy*, not *Three Men & A Baby*.

My explanation went something like, "It's 9:30 p.m. now, but we will land at 6:00 a.m., which is 5:00 a.m., which is 2:00 a.m. in Las Vegas."

Each time I spoke, smoke billowed from their ears. I hope my explanation didn't initiate an early onset of Alzheimer's disease at row six; I bet that requires an irregularity report.

The cute old guy in 1B began setting his watch before we left the gate in Las Vegas, and when we were flying somewhere over Louisiana, he still hadn't set his watch. While I sat in the jumpseat, I watched him from the top of my glasses. I felt terrible and fought back the urge to throw the watch away in the trash bin and save him the frustration, but it looked like a decent watch.

The three blue hairs in 1D, E, and F were extremely loud. And the one in 1D was driving me fucking nuts, "Joe, can you pour my tomato juice? Joe, does this have low sodium? I can't have a lot of salt. My doctor says…"

"Joe, I can't find my bottle of water," 1E said.

And 1D followed up, "Joe, What time are we landing?"

My concern wasn't about their tomato juice or their lost water; it was about 1F who looked dead slumped against the window sleeping. I consider getting the AED down and placing it by the aisle when 1E said, "Never mind, Joe. I found my water. Everything is fine."

The bald guy in 2D stared at me all night. His girlfriend was sleeping next to him. He was super hot, so I asked him, "Hey man, do you want a beer?"

He shook his head no. I assumed a hand job was out of the question.

It was stuffy and warm on the airplane, probably the heat escaping everyone over the age of 90. The passenger in 11D walked up to the front galley of the aircraft and complained about the heat for the second time. With his shirt halfway unbuttoned, he said, "I'd love to take my shirt off, but I know I can't."

"Yeah," I responded, "I'd leave my shirt on."

Actually, in the horrible lighting, he looked kind of buff. My outside voice said NO, but my inside voice said YES. I should have told him to take it off, and if my eyes started burning from his heinous chest, I'd just tell him it's against FAA regulations for ugly chested people to walk around shirtless on a red-eye to Ft. Lauderdale.

When our flight landed in Ft. Lauderdale, it took forever for the passengers to deplane. Forever. It's March, and I felt like I was going to be standing in that galley until my next birthday, which is in fucking November.

The old passengers who needed wheelchairs in the first few rows — and there were many — stood up and questioned why the wheelchairs were not ready. I had announced for anyone needing a wheelchair to remain seated until the last passengers were off the airplane, but they most likely had their hearing aids off.

They started getting nasty and verbalizing about why they shouldn't have to wait for wheelchairs, but I turned my head and ignored them. It was too early in the morning for me to argue with these passengers, but because I am who I am, I also love correcting people when the opportunity presents itself. A few times I reminded 1E and 1D that the other 140 passengers on the airplane should not have to wait until they crawl down the aisle to get to the jet bridge and into the wheelchairs. Seriously, I know they don't have much time left on the planet, but goddamn, they can wait another 15 minutes until the walking passengers step off the airplane.

One lady seated in row two started pushing my early morning time change button."Last week," she spoke, "they told us we'd get off the airplane first,"

I smiled knowing that no flight attendant, gate agent — or pilot — on planet Earth, ever relayed that information to her. She must have been confused about deplaning first and being seated first at Black Angus on a Sunday afternoon.

I politely said, "I don't know who told you that, but they gave you wrong information."

She looked at me cross-eyed. Or maybe she had a mini-stroke. I don't know. All I know is that this shows how selfish people can be no matter what age.

Fort Lauderdale is God's Waiting Room. The city should rename their airport to God's Waiting Room/ Hollywood International Airport and Wheelchair Depot.

Journal Entry: Easter Weekend

Dear Journal,

It's Saturday, and I commuted to LAX early this morning. Why did I pick up a trip over Easter Sunday? Yes, I'm an atheist, but you don't have to believe in God to take a holiday off. I don't believe in Santa Claus, and I love tearing open Christmas presents.

When I walked onto the airplane in San Francisco, a male passenger seated across from me yelled, "You're Flight Attendant Joe from Instagram."

I nodded, "Yes I am."

We had a brief conversation and then I went back to reading the news on my cell phone. Now that this guy knows where I work, I might have to kill him. That's a joke. Well, maybe just gouge his eyes out so he can't point me out in a flight attendant line up. It's weird being noticed by strangers. I know I throw myself out there for social media to judge, but when I meet someone in person, I'm timid. Every time. I guess that's a good thing. Am I humble? That can't be it. My husband says I don't know how to be humble. I think that's an insult, but I've gotten comfortable with my lifestyle, so I let shit like that slide off my back. Not a good enough reason to seek a lawyer. Not yet, anyway.

Maybe it's me keeping my ego in check. That's difficult for me. Always a struggle with the ego. Oprah Winfrey was right; egos are hard to manage.

Did she say that?

She may have, she says a lot.

I'm working with Laura, who is one of my favorite flight attendants in the entire world. Scratch that, solar system. She's an actor and will be on an episode of a major ABC television show next week. Every time I see her, I ask her the same question, why are you handing out Sprites and doing safety demonstrations on an airplane when you are guest starring on a major network television show? She's on television. Not just a Premarin commercial, but on ABC. She's clearly not sleeping with enough directors. Well, she's probably sleeping with enough directors — Lord knows I would — but not the right ones. There's a difference. I'd have my legs up on a casting couch so often I'd rub the hair off my ass. Probably be best to carry around an extra sofa so not to catch herpes. I don't know if that's how you contract Hollywood herpes, but I'm not taking any chances, and it's always best to think ahead. What if the *Kate Plus 8* mom auditioned on the same sofa where I received my ass pounding? We can't have that. I don't love Hollywood that much. But Laura is amazing. Did I say that already? Perfection! She's hot and lets me touch her ass.

SPOILER: it felt like a rock.

We banter and have the best comedic timing together. We go back and forth like the Olsen twins fighting over a cigarette. It's that intense. I say something snarky to her and then she comes right back with a quick response. And the best part is we do it in front of passengers.

At one point, Laura walked up to me while I was charging a passenger for his drink. She said, "I wanna do one with you." She was talking about taking payment from a passenger with our new electronic devices, but I went a step further.

I spun around like a teen on ecstasy, "I've been waiting to do it with you since we met."

The passenger loved it. He told us to keep going, but I think the guy was getting sexually aroused. That's most likely why he asked for extra napkins.

There was an entire family of six on the flight heading to Orlando for a week at Disney World. That's nothing new, but they were happy and joking, which was odd. Most families heading to Disney have a divorce lawyer on speed dial. Or, if they have money, they pack them in their carry-on luggage.

The two lovely ladies in 1D and 1F gave each of us — me, Laura, and Barbara — a box of Easter chocolates. So thoughtful and made me feel all warm and tingly inside. The pilots were alright, but on a quick stop in Houston, they ran off the airplane to get food and didn't offer to get us anything. We had no time to get food because it was a quick turnaround flight and we had to start boarding immediately. When they walked on with their plastic bags filled with barbecue food, I snapped, "Thanks for asking us if we need any food."

The older first officer said, "You can have some of mine."

I exclaimed, "You bitches!" and walked to the back of the airplane. Talk about being selfish. I wonder if they will report me? To be honest, I'm not concerned, the first officer was clocking my jock the entire flight. He's 59 years oldish. Nice enough, but not my type. They rarely are. When we first met, he gay waved at me and said something flirty, but I blocked it out of my mind. I honestly don't remember. Laura asked me how I fit inside the flight deck with him when it was time for the pilots to take a lavatory break. He's heavyset, and not the cute type of heavyset, he's heavyset where a bunch of his friends invited him to play basketball, and he confused the word "play" with "eat." It looks like he swallowed a basketball. I simply told her, "On my knees, with my head in his lap." We both laughed. She gets me, every ounce of my filthy mouth. I wasn't even going to go inside the flight deck because I feared he'd want me to play with one of the balls he was carrying around.

We landed in Orlando, and my friend Willis picked all three of us up for drinks. He's upgrading to captain. He deserves it. One of my favorite pilots. He's sweet, friendly to flight attendants, and handsome. I'd do him in a second, but he's not into sword fighting with male flight attendants. And he's married. I've offered to do him and his wife, but I think they're pretty adamant about not having a third. Their loss.

It's Easter Sunday. It amazes me that Jesus Christ came back to life, pushed a heavy-ass boulder out of the way, and ascended into heaven, but I can't get the bitch in 27C to shut off her laptop after I've asked her nicely three times. I bet if Zombie Jesus walked up and told her to shut off her computer, she'd have no problem. Sure, Zombie Jesus. Whatever you say, Zombie Jesus. Would you like me to swap you my aisle seat for your middle seat, Zombie Jesus? You know it's sad when Zombie Jesus gets more respect than the trained flight attendant. It's not like passengers can't turn their laptops back on after the airplane hits 10,000 feet. Do passengers just hate following a few simple rules? There's an easy answer for that: walk. These people don't have to be on an airplane, like I said, they can walk. Put some shoes on and use those two legs that Zombie Jesus gave you.

Our first leg was ridiculous. The passengers were rowdy. Puerto Ricans from Orlando, so that says it all. I lived in Orlando for 25 years, so I am quite fluent in Puerto Rican behavior. I had a saying when I lived in Orlando; it went something like, "I've reached my PRM." What's PRM? No, it's not a new form of birth control —although it sure sounds like it, and Puerto Ricans could use all the help they can get when it comes to not procreating — but it stands for Puerto Rican Max. The number of Puerto Ricans any individual can manage in a given day. Everyone's number is different. While white Republicans might only be able to handle two Puerto Ricans in a day, my number goes into the triple digits. I'd say 200. That's about it. Any more and I lose my fucking patience. Back in 2012, that one acronym got my blog reported to my airline by a fellow flight attendant. I know who reported me and I'm patiently awaiting the day I can trip her as she runs through the airport. I've said it once, and I'll repeat it — flight attendants are shady bitches. They will throw you under the airplane tire faster than you can say, "Are we delayed?"

One thing I've learned since moving to California is that Mexicans are better neighbors than Puerto Ricans. I'm sorry, but it's true. Mexicans are hard working, quiet, and respectful; I don't care what the GOP says. Sure, they're probably quiet because they're illegals and don't want to bring attention to themselves, but I don't blame them… and I don't care. I'd willingly stand in line waiting to get out of Tijuana with 1,000 Mexicans than work one flight to San Juan. Puerto Ricans are out of control, especially in Florida. If you've visited Florida once, you know what I mean. On a recent layover in Orlando, I was walking down the street during the day — minding my own business — when a car full of Puerto Ricans drove by yelling homosexual slurs at me from their window. I wasn't even sucking dick, just walking down the street. Can you imagine what they might have said if I was sucking dick on the corner? I don't know, but it would probably be hot. But seriously, do you know how many times I've walked down the street in California and been harassed by a Mexican? Zero. Nada. Well, except for that time I yelled at some Mexican for riding his bike on the sidewalk.

I think I harassed him, so never mind.

All the passengers were demanding and seated in coach. Coach passengers pay less for their tickets but require the most. I'll never understand that. First class passengers rarely need anything. Ask someone in the back of the airplane on an Orlando flight what they want to drink, and they'll order a Sprite, OJ, and coffee with 27 sugars. Now that I think about it, I guess it's like that on all flights, but today it seemed much worse.

At least I had Laura with me, my knight and shining blue-rimmed glasses. She's the type of flight attendant I miss when she's in the front galley, and I'm in the back. We smiled and waved at each other down the aisle of the airplane. She takes my breath away. If only she had a penis, I'd let her penetrate me every day of the week.

The flight from Houston to Los Angeles was calmer than the Orlando to Houston flight. Dropped off all the Orlando passengers in Houston, so the next group was a little more polite. You know, no poking your ass or hissing at you like an angry cobra. Sounds terrible, but it's the absolute fucking truth. Ask any flight attendant. I'm just brave enough to say it out loud or jot it down in my journal. Honestly, I may be guilty of saying it in the galley under moments of distress.

We swapped out pilots in Houston, and I recognized our new first officer. He commuted on my plane a few weeks ago, and I found him quite attractive. Not hot, but cute. Something handsome and wholesome about him. During the lavatory break, I was inside the flight deck, and he said, "How did you get on the cover of that flight attendant magazine?" Did I forget to mention that I was on the cover of our department magazine? It happened a few months ago. It's not so much a magazine as a few sheets of paper stapled together — but it was still cool. I love when people recognize me from that cover. There's a new magazine out now, and I'm not too happy about that. Me and my ego. As I've said, I understand Oprah's ego; I just don't know why she needs such a large front yard.

I should have tried some dirty talk with the first officer, but I decided to talk about the blog.

He asked, "Do you ever get in trouble with the airline?" The answer is always no, so far.

I'm awaiting the day that management calls me into the office and asks, "Are you Flight Attendant Joe?" I've thought long and hard about my response and practiced it countless times in front of the mirror. It's perfect, and I'm quite proud of it.

"Que? Hablo penga." I have no idea if they will buy it, but I think it's pure genius. Basically, blah blah blah, something about speaking in a penis language. Like speaking in tongues, but with cock. I figured if I'm addressing flight attendant management, I should talk in a language they understand.

And most of them understand dick.

The second question the pilot asked was, "Do you make any money from the blog?"

My response, "Not enough to quit this fucking shit hole." Or something like that. I figured if I am addressing pilots inside the flight deck, I should talk in a language they understand. And all pilots think airlines are shit holes.

The way he stared at me struck me odd as if he was looking directly into my soul. I can't lie, I almost busted a nut all over the back of the captain's chair.

He shared, "I've been married for 13 years."

I acted shocked, "13 years? Did you get married when you were 12?"

He loved that. He smirked, and I almost needed the emergency oxygen tank. The captain was outside in the galley chatting with the older flight attendant, Barbara. I could see Laura on the camera in the back galley. I couldn't wait to tell her about how I almost nutted in my polyester pants inside the flight deck. She'd understand. She'd probably hold my hand and talk me through it.

When the flight deck door finally opened, I stepped out into the galley and Barbara was practically foaming at the mouth. At first, I worried she had an old lady stroke, but then I realized she was just a pilot slut. An old-fashioned pilot slut. They're obviously still around. She pushed the trash bin back into place and whispered, "He's such a handsome man."

I smiled, "Yeah, he's alright. You should try and get you some."

She laughed, "Oh stop, Joe."

Barbara was in her mid-fifties and needing a good pounding of the century. She's surpassed cobwebs. Poor thing probably calls her pussy, Barbara's Web.

Customer Service Goes Both Ways

As I made my way through John F. Kennedy International Airport with my coworker Lana, I kept thinking about the hot male passenger seated in 1F on my flight from Los Angeles the night before. He was adorable. Scruffy face. Nice and polite. The kind of guy you could never bring home for dinner because your mom would fuck him in your childhood bedroom. Then you'd have to stab your mom for being a slut. Seriously, he was stab-your-whore-mother sexy.

Then Lana distracted me from hot guys and whore mothers, "I think that's Paula Abdul in those black boots."

"What? Where?" I spun around like someone kicked my ass, "Oh my god. I'll be right back."

I immediately recognized her by the Jamba Juice; it wasn't difficult because she moved extremely slow for someone who sang a song titled, "Rush Rush". She apparently didn't pay attention to the lyrics; she sauntered through the airport like she sang, Delay Delay. When I walk through the airport, I act like I'm being chased by Scientologists trying to make me hold those truth cans, or whatever the hell they are. I sprinted past Paula by 10 feet, turned around, we made eye contact, and I almost threw myself at her feet and confessed my past teenage love for her.

Holy shit! Paula Abdul and I straight up made eye contact. I instinctively wanted to download all her songs and listen to them as I danced through the airport for the rest of the night…but I had a flight to work.

Once my new best friend Paula and I made eye contact, I put my head down and acted like I was looking for my departure gate. I may have even said, "Where am I going?" to throw her and any other nosy passenger listening — or watching me stalk Paula by the Jamba Juice — off. Paula looked amazing. The only thing that could top that experience would have been "Cold Hearted" playing throughout the airport.

After my run-in with Paula Abdul, I hightailed my ass to the gate only to find out that my flight to Orlando was full. Not only was the flight full, but we also had over 20 standby passengers listed.

When the gate agent finished telling me the stats of the flight, I politely added, "There are like 10 open seats on the other delayed flight to Orlando. Why not move these standbys over to that flight?"

That annoyed him, "I'm too busy for that."

How airlines win any awards with attitudes like that is a fucking mystery.

During boarding, I noticed that the Columbia University baseball team was on our flight. They were all sexy college guys. So hot. Extremely hot. After the last one boarded and took his seat, I had to confirm whether the water in the front galley was from my excitement or the snow outside.

Just to confirm, it was snow.

While waiting for the gate agent to bring down the final paperwork, I noticed a chubby lady in 3A staring at me. The way she looked through me made me extremely uncomfortable. Did she want some dick? That was my first thought. Listen, I'm not against screwing a chick, but she has to be hot — I have to be extremely intoxicated — and I'd prefer her not being a lady bear from Orlando.

While I paced in the galley figuring out how to repel her sexual advances, she rang her call bell. Hesitating, I walked over. Something told me she was aroused and probably cemented to the seat. I've heard of that happening. Women not wearing underwear and being so turned on by their flight attendant that they become suctioned to their chair, unable to break free until the airplane cools down. If that were the case, I'd have to call maintenance to remove her from the aircraft.

I stepped over to her row and shut off the call light, "May I help you?"

She licked her lips, and my balls retreated into my stomach. Lucky for me, and the guy sitting next to her, she was not looking to make a meal out of my crotch. She smiled, "Can I get up and use the lavatory?"

I was relieved, and my balls flopped back down to their natural home. I smiled, "Of course. Just be quick, we're about to close the door."

After the flight took off, I logged onto the internet to check the status of our return flight back to New York. We were changing out pilots once we landed in Orlando and I needed to find out what flight they were currently on. A great lead flight attendant knows when there's a pilot crew change; an excellent lead flight attendant knows when to expect them at the gate.

Sadly, their status would not help us out anytime soon. Our pilot's flight was canceled in Newark. As I placed my cell phone down on the galley counter, I shook my head realizing there was a high probability that our night might turn into a complete and utter clusterfuck. I'm no fortune teller, but I've been a flight attendant long enough to see a shit show coming from 1,000 miles away.

To change up the negativity in my brain about what was heading our way when we landed in Orlando, I posted a comment on the Flight Attendant Joe Facebook page about the baseball players. It read: *Columbia baseball team on my flight. Hot. I can barely contain myself. Air Traffic Control, we've got a boner! I repeat we've got a boner en route to Orlando.*

What I neglected to remember was that I had linked my Flight Attendant Joe Facebook page to my Twitter account, which promptly posted the comment on Twitter.

About an hour later, not thinking any further about my social media post, Lana walked up to me in the galley while I poured a cup of coffee and smirked, "Did you post something on Twitter about hot baseball players?"

I was caught off guard, "Yes. How do you know?"

She giggled, "Well, one of the guys in the back found the tweet and showed me his phone and asked, 'Is that the flight attendant up front?'"

Shocked. I stood there for a brief moment wondering how I'd get out of this fiasco. I have always expected that one day something I say on my blog — or book — would come back to bite me in the ass, but never did I think it would be from hot baseball players. Typically, that would be incredible. On the airplane I was slightly nervous, I'd be getting my ass kicked up and down the aisle until we landed. I kept my distance from the back half of the airplane.

"I'm not going back there unless you or Maria are dying, and I can't even guarantee I'll come back there for that."

Lana erupted into a cackle, "Joe, they're cool about it. They think it's great. Trust me; they won't say anything to you."

She lied, but in a positive way. A few of them said something to me as they walked off the airplane. A few thanked me, a few smiled, and one of the player's girlfriends hugged me as she stepped into the front galley.

Here I had expected to have my ass handed to me by big beefy baseball players, but it was quite the opposite. When I finally logged into my Twitter account, I noticed that three of the baseball players retweeted my tweet and five liked it. With all the sensitive and easily offended people running around the country, it's nice to interact with strangers who have a sense of humor.

I love baseball players.

Once everyone deplaned, Lana, Maria, and I made our way off the airplane and found a quiet spot behind the gate to camp out while waiting for Crew Scheduling to anal rape us. Sorry, what I meant to say was, find us available pilots to fly the airplane.

As the lead flight attendant, I had to find out what the hell was going on. It was 9:45 pm and we were scheduled to do a quick turn back to JFK. What's a quick turn? I knew you'd ask. A quick turn is when the airline gives the crew barely enough time to deplane all the passengers, clean the airplane, board the new passengers, and depart for the next destination. If we need food, our problem. If we need a quick lavatory break, better hold it until the airplane levels off at 38,000 feet.

We sat behind gate 112 with no gate agent in sight. No smiling face, or grimace, waiting to greet us and give us an update on our departing flight. Waiting for gate agents is not unusual in the airline industry. Gate agents are notorious for reporting flight attendants for being a minute late, but then act like it's acceptable for themselves to go missing in action when the opportunity presents itself. It's a battle that has been raging since the days of Amelia Earhart. I wouldn't be surprised if she and her copilot went missing because a gate agent wasn't there to wave her down to the right beach.

In the airline industry, it's eat or be eaten. And tonight, I was hungry as fuck.

I stormed over to gate 114 where I saw three gate agents cutting up and chuckling about who-knows-what. That immediately irritated me. "Hey, what's going on?"

They stopped laughing and looked at me like I had walked in on them having a threesome. I continued, "We just came in on flight 76. We don't have pilots to fly us back to JFK. Do you know what's going on?"

The female with spiky blond hair addressed me, "The earlier JFK still hasn't departed. They're either canceling that flight or your flight. We don't know yet."

"Do they have any pilots?"

All three of them shook their head, but Spiky responded, "Nope. They're short pilots tonight."

"What should we do?" I asked fishing for additional feedback.

"I don't know. Stand over by the gate. We'll let you know when we knowing something."

That's not the type of professionalism I expect from my airline. I had whiplash from our back and forth. I needed a few Vicodin for the pain.

Actually, I needed a few Vicodin because they are amazing and make challenging situations better.

When I walked back to gate 112, there was an entirely new level of drama waiting for me, and that drama was Teddy.

"Joe. What the hell's up? Why's the flight delayed?"

I could smell the alcohol emitting from his pores. "We're waiting for pilots."

"You working it?" His words came out slurred with a side of saliva.

"Yes, Teddy, I am. You alright?" I sat down behind the glass wall separating the counter from the seating area. Lana and Maria walked off to get food, and I was stuck managing Teddy.

Teddy was beyond wasted. On a scale of 1 to 10 (10 being shit-faced), he was a 13. Now, don't get me wrong, flight attendants are allowed to have fun and let loose when they travel for personal reasons. Trust me; I've had my share of fun during personal travel, but even though Teddy was in civilian clothes, he was traveling for business. He wasn't on vacation in Orlando, he was part of the Standard Advisory Team and happened to be in Orlando conducting meetings with management. The thought of him being this intoxicated at the gate made me nervous.

I will confess, I have no room to talk about being drunk while conducting business on behalf of the airline. Many years ago, when I was on the Standard Advisory Team, I drank too much at a work function dinner in Miami. That night, so long ago, I haphazardly grabbed the bus microphone and roasted the hell out of the vice president of our department. She took it all in stride and didn't rip my wings off me, but when I think back to that night, I say to myself, what's wrong with you, Joe? Alcohol is a fantastic drug. My career might have ended that night if it weren't for at least one smart, sober, and professional coworker who walked up to the front of the bus and removed the microphone from my hand and directed me to an empty seat.

Who puts a microphone on a bus with drunk people on it? It's brilliant but extremely dangerous for career advancement.

But this situation with Teddy was different. When I was an intoxicated fool, I was on a chartered bus — with other drunk flight attendants — and far from angry gate agents and the prying eyes of frustrated passengers. Teddy was drunk for the entire Orlando International Airport to see and now I was responsible for the outcome.

"How much have you had to drink?"

"Enough," he sputtered out and plopped down in the chair next to me. "This bitchy gate agent is done with me. She told me to step away from the gate, or she's gonna report me."

"You better listen to her," and then I whispered, "Bitch, you're drunk."

I didn't need this bullshit plus a delay. Teddy continued, "Would you deny me boarding because I've had some drinks?"

At that exact moment, a family came and sat to the side of us, so I had to whisper even softer, "No, but you need to settle down because you're going to get in so much trouble. Go get some food and drink some water before the flight."

"You're not my mother."

"Teddy, get some food or you're gonna get kicked off the flight and end up in Orlando for the night."

I stood up to greet a few passengers who walked up to the gate. It was a good reason to step away from Teddy so he'd walk away and get food.

"Can I help you?"

"Is the flight delayed?" A woman asked while holding a child in her arms.

"I'm sorry, I don't have much information," then I looked over at gate 114 and pointed, "but those three gate agents over there will be able to answer all your questions."

That one passenger who walked up to the gate caused a tsunami of questions from concerned passengers. Why is the flight delayed? Will this flight go out before the earlier one? Do you have pilots? Are you going to cancel? Who can I speak to about a free upgrade? Why doesn't this airline have enough pilots? Will we get free drinks for being delayed?

I answered their questions to the best of my ability without telling anyone to drop dead. It's an accomplishment I pat myself on the back for to this day.

I felt a sense of relaxation as the last passenger walked away towards gate 114, but my anxiety intensified when

Teddy strolled up with a bag of food from McDonald's. We sat back down beside each other, and as he placed a few french fries in his mouth, he aggressively asked, "You used to be fun. What happened to you?"

Never do I get offended, but this disturbed me, "I'm still fun, but I'm in my uniform and dealing with a shitty night."

Ignoring me, "I want another beer."

I put my arm on the back of the chair between us, "I'd have to disagree with that. You need water and to chill or you're gonna get fired." I stood up, "I need to use the restroom. You ok?"

He barely heard me, "I'm not getting fired. I run this airline. Do you hear me? I've got these people wrapped around my finger."

That was enough for me. If Teddy didn't want to help himself, I gave up trying. I shrugged my shoulders and headed towards the restroom. After my restroom break, I saw him sitting at the airport bar — beer in hand — chatting with another airline employee.

I was jealous.

At 11:25 p.m., we still had no information on the status of our flight and no pilots. I walked back over to gate 114 and politely asked Spiky, "Have you found out anything?"

"Oh yeah, your flight's been canceled."

"What? Really? When did you find that out?"

"A few minutes ago, they could only find two pilots able to work. They're moving all the passengers from your flight to this one."

I walked back to gate 112 and updated Lana and Maria. The three of us had this dazed and confused look on our face about what was happening. I dialed Crew Scheduling, and a scheduler finally answered after I sat on hold for 15 minutes. It was a brief phone call, "Hi, this is Joe Thomas, employee number 01972. Our flight canceled in Orlando. Do you want us to deadhead on the flight to JFK that will be leaving shortly?"

He paused for a moment, "Hi Joe, can we call you right back?"

I spoke up, "We don't have time. The flight will start boarding soon. Are we deadheading on it?"

Again, "We're going to have to call you right back."

I hung up my phone and looked at Lana and Maria, "They're going to call us back."

The idea of them calling us right back sounded highly unlikely. While we patiently waited for that callback, we sat to the side of the gate and watched the other flight attendants board the airplane to complete their security checks. We watched the pilots arrive from their New Orleans flight and board the flight. We watched the passengers board the airplane, drunk Teddy stumble onto the airplane, and the gate agents close the aircraft door. Then we finally stood up and walked away once the plane pulled away from the jet bridge and taxied to the runway without us.

We shuffled our feet and headed towards the flight attendant lounge. Maria said jokingly, "We're stranded at the airport."

It wasn't a joke. It was the truth.

At 1:30 a.m. I became enraged. What do you expect? We were exhausted, and poor communication from crew scheduling left us stranded in Orlando. Did I say poor communication? That's not right, how about zero communication? We waited over two hours for a phone call that never came. The three of us sat at a round table in the flight attendant lounge trying to make light of the situation, but as each minute clicked over, my incredible sense of humor waned.

"I'm calling them back. This has gone on long enough."

Lana added, "They forgot about us. They don't even know where we are."

I dialed the number and sat on hold for what seemed like hours. It got to the point where I could recite the entire hold message until finally, I heard the line ring and someone picked up. "This is Crew Scheduling, may I help you?"

I dove into the story giving as much detail as possible. When airlines face operational obstacles, it's a domino effect that hits the rest of us. And when there are flight delays and cancellations, our lifeline — Crew Scheduling — fails miserably. That's not an exaggeration. Abusive foster parents tend to be more caring than the people behind those telephones.

I wrapped up my explanation of being left stranded at the airport, and was completely surprised by the response from the scheduler on the other end of the phone. The scheduler evenly said, "Oh yeah. That was me you talked to."

It took all my energy not to assault him over the phone. My body became overheated, and my forehead began to sweat. Lana and Maria stared at me from across the table wondering what was causing the steam to radiate off my bald head. Lava was ready to spew out of my nose, ears, eyeballs, mouth, and rectum.

To be fair, that usually happens when I eat spicy chicken wings.

Taking a deep breath, I asked, "Why haven't you called me back?"

I honestly can't remember what he said, but I guarantee you that it was a shitty excuse. No excuse justifies leaving three flight attendants stranded at the airport for over four hours. Maybe I'd have forgiven him and his awful communication skills if he shared with me that our headquarters building had burnt to the ground and he was taking my call from a pay phone across the street while a group of homeless people pissed all over him.

I'm not saying I would have, just maybe.

Disappointed. The scheduler's accent was so thick I never got his name. It sounded like he had been born on a distant planet and grew up in Scotland. I had to guess his name. Rian? Or was it Rule? Maybe it was Root? Listen, I didn't give a damn who he was or what his name was; he could have been a member of the *Guardians of the Galaxy* for all I cared, I just want to know what the endgame was for my flight attendants and me.

In Root's heavy accent he informed me, "I'm sorry, we're busy. But we're getting you a hotel room for tonight and booking your flights back to Los Angeles for tomorrow."

I kept quiet while he continued, "We will fly you from Orlando to Boston then to LA."

I interrupted, "Why make us fly all the way up to Boston and then to LA? That's out of the way. We should be back at base by 4 p.m. tomorrow. That will get us back to base at 9 p.m. Just book us from Orlando to Houston and then on to LA."

"There is no enough connection time."

How does this guy work in scheduling and not understand how the airplanes flow? Alright, it's not his job to know every route the airline offers, but it's always a good idea that before you speak, you should know what the hell you are talking about.

"It's the same airplane." I shook my head at Lana and Maria.

"The same airplane?"

"Yes, it's the same airplane."

"Would you hold for a minute?"And the hold music began playing in my ear.

I assume that there's a secret rulebook that crew schedulers follow when they answer a flight attendant call. There's probably a rule book for pilots too, but their rulebook likely consists of three simple sentences:

1. Don't argue with the pilots

2. Don't place pilots on hold

3. Give them anything they want, or they will strike

With flight attendants, it's more complicated. During crew scheduler training, I imagine schedulers watch countless videos and spend hours of role-playing to perfect placing a flight attendant on hold. It doesn't matter how long the call is — whether it's 10 seconds or 10 minutes — you will at some point be placed on hold. No question about it. If you dial the crew scheduling number, your ass will be swaying to Muzak while waiting for them to return to the phone.

I expect there's a list taped to each desk with guidelines for answering a flight attendant call. It probably looks something like this:

1. Say hello in an unpleasant tone

2. Listen, but do not offer any assistance

3. Put flight attendant on hold

4. When you return to the call, say NO!

5. Tell them to follow up with their union rep

6. Hang up

While I stared at Lana and fantasized about the assumed list, Root came back on the phone, "Joe. Yes. We'll book you through Houston tomorrow. You are all set. Anything else I can help you with?"

"What about our hotel rooms for tonight?"

"Oh yes. May I call you back?"

I chuckled, "Absolutely not. You've already forgotten to call us once," I wanted this guy feeling as guilty as possible, "so just put me on hold, and we'll make our way up to the terminal."

"Okay Joe, I understand."

The Muzak started, and I stood up, "Alright ladies, he's getting our hotel room. Let's head upstairs."

Maria was thrilled, "Finally. I'm exhausted."

The three of us stepped into the elevator, and the unthinkable happened. No, an airplane did not crash into the airport and strike the elevator, that would have been manageable. It's much much worse than that — I lost cell phone reception.

Panic-stricken, I hurled myself out of the elevator when the door opened. I redialed crew scheduling, but because of the high call volume going on — at 2:00 a.m.? — I spent a solid 20 minutes trying to speak to another human being. I get that they are busy, I honestly do, but having three flight attendants left helpless in an airport for almost five hours is bad management. Without sounding too dramatic, it's almost right up there with Donald Trump throwing paper towels at Puerto Ricans after the destruction of their island.

I said almost. I hope the United States government at least splurged for the two-ply.

I don't mean to bitch about crew scheduling. It's a tough job, and that department has the highest turn over rate in the industry. Can you imagine taking calls from frustrated flight attendants and pilots all day? I'd sooner stand under the airplane and clean the shitters. It makes sense why they quit so often. But for those who do stay and continue collecting a paycheck, they have a job to do, and that job is making sure flight attendants and pilots are taken care of while flying around the country. My responsibility is to serve nuts and Diet Cokes to demanding passengers. Crew Schedulings job is to book hotel rooms and schedule van service for needy flight attendants.

Whether crew scheduling wants to accept it or not, flight attendants are their customers. Their single function during the workday is providing service to flight attendants and pilots. Just like airline passengers are our customers, we are crew schedulings customers. Something tells me that point was left out during their initial training. Or maybe it wasn't, and they just forgot. Thankfully, I'm here to reiterate it — WE ARE THEIR CUSTOMER!

When a customer has an issue with a company, and they contact the customer service hotline number, they don't expect poor treatment. That's how I feel when calling crew scheduling. Whenever I reach out to them to resolve work-related issues, I am pleasant and respectful on the telephone. I am not rude, and because of that, I expect them to be cheery and ready to help me out. I want them to do their job. It's not my responsibility if they are having a stressful day. I've had countless stressful days on the airplane, and because I am providing customer service to the passengers, I am not allowed to let it affect their experience. I want crew scheduling to treat me like I treat that cute little old lady who can't reach her carry on bag in the overhead bin, with importance and consideration.

Customer service goes both ways; the airline expects us to provide award-winning customer service to our passengers, we should expect it from the employees in crew scheduling.

My patience lost, I verbally exploded while the three of us sat in chairs under the airport rotunda, "Why isn't this guy calling me back? It's not like he doesn't have my phone number," I said to Lana. "They can surely find my number when they need to change my schedule."

Lana and Maria shook their heads in agreement.

Maria sat up and grabbed her phone, "This is ridiculous. Let me see if I can get through to them." I thanked her for trying while I continued on hold.

Within minutes, Maria's phone began ringing through to a crew scheduler. I practically snatched the phone out of her hand. It was Root; I was void of any niceties. "Root? It's Joe. Why didn't you call me back when you realized I wasn't on the other end?"

"I've been trying to find you a hotel."

Trying?

He continued, "We've called 14 hotels. There are no hotel rooms available in Orlando."

"Why did you stop at 14?"

"What?" He sounded perplexed.

"Why did you stop at 14? You should keep looking, right?"

He was taken aback by my bluntness, "We are still trying, but it doesn't look good,' he stuttered into the phone. He was having a stressful night — so were we — but at least he had a pillow to place his head on at the end of his shift.

I refused to back down, "There are thousands of hotel rooms in Orlando. I lived in Orlando for 25 years; there are more hotel rooms here than in Las Vegas."

"Joe. I don't know what to do."

I laughed my maniacal laugh. I'm proud of my crazy laughter, it usually lasts about 15 seconds and happens when I've reached the end of my rope. It's the laugh that scares people and is a good indication that I am about to cut someone. When I finished laughing, I confirmed, "I just want you to know that I am laughing, but this is not funny."

I stayed as calm as possible. Sure, my crazy laugh came out, but I had no plans on stabbing anyone. Also, all calls with crew scheduling are recorded and losing my cool would not be helpful.

He continued insisting that there were no hotel rooms available in Orlando. I pushed back that he was not looking hard enough.

"Can you hold for a minute?"

"Yes, I'll be right here."

I have had better customer service experiences with the cable company then I was having at that moment with my airline. In less than a minute, he was back on the phone, "We can get you all at three separate hotels in Orlando."

I repeated his offer out loud, but Lana and Maria shared their displeasure with that idea. I shut it down. "No. We should be at the same hotel."

"There's nothing available."

My frustration and fatigue finally caught up with me, "At this point, it doesn't matter where you send us. We just need three hotel rooms at the same hotel. What that means is, I don't care how much the airline has to spend on these rooms, we just need to go to bed."

He put me on hold again, and my mind felt numb. My watch read 2:15 a.m. and I realized that we had been sitting in the airport since 9:45 p.m. Six hours of no direction and poor management. That's what it must have felt like working on the Hillary Clinton campaign.

Miraculously, in less than five minutes, he tracked down three rooms at the Hyatt Regency on International Drive. I was so excited and relieved I held myself back from promising oral the next time I was at JFK. Instantly, I forgave him for leaving us homeless at the airport. As he relayed the hotel information, I repeated it while Maria jotted it down.

"Alright, Mr. Joe. I apologize for forgetting to call you back. Are we good?"

"Yes. We're good…" then I realized something important, "wait one second, what about transportation? Where are they picking us up?"

"Transportation? I didn't think of that."

And just like that, I hated Root again.

I politely asked, "What do you mean you didn't think of that? How are we supposed to get to the hotel? We need transportation set up."

He repeated, "Transportation?" as if he assumed flight attendants always walk to the hotel. I held my breath waiting for him to continue, "I don't know. There's no transportation scheduled to the hotel. Can you take a taxi?"

At least he didn't put me back on hold. "Yes. We'll take a taxi, and I'll expense it when I'm back in Los Angeles."

Lana and Maria stared at me like two lost children while I threw my hands up in the air expressing my frustration with the entire night.

Off the hook, Root cheered up, "That's great. I'll make sure you have a shuttle van in the morning."

"What time?" I question.

Again, he was stumped. I paused for a moment fighting off the urge to throw my cell phone across the empty airport. Instead of giving Root anymore of my energy, I came up with the quickest solution, "Just send me an email with what time the van will be picking us up. Is that okay?

"Yes. That's perfect," I could hear the relief in Root's voice, "thank you so much, Joe. I'm sorry about all this."

Without responding, I hung up the call and reached for my tote bag. "I'm so done. We've gotta catch a taxi."

They jumped up from the uncomfortable airport chairs with what I can only imagine was their last ounce of energy. "Thank goodness you are working, Joe," Maria said, "I don't have the money for a taxi."

Lana piped in. "This is wrong. Making us pay for our ride. I don't have that kinda money, either."

We continued towards the escalator abreast, "No worries. I'm just ready for bed." I looked at my watch, "Three o'clock in the morning. It's ridiculous."

We hailed a taxi at the baggage claim, and I send Trick Daddy a text message: *We got so fucked tonight. In a cab heading to the hotel in Orlando. What's up?*

He texted back within a minute: *We were three hours delayed into LA. We're waiting for the fucking hotel van. It's all bullshit.*

I sighed deeply. Not to sound like a total bitch, but it's quite nice knowing that your friend is getting screwed over at the same time you are. We continued to bitch back and forth via text, which felt right at the moment but ended up being more toxic than cat shit.

When I am frustrated, I feel the urge to vent and complain about whatever is causing me conflict. I am not alone in that practice. Most human beings spend their days grumbling about stupid shit, instead of merely letting trivial matters roll off their backs like raindrops. That seems like the more natural option — just say fuck it and move on — but sadly, our brains usually take the more difficult choice. The possibility of working ourselves into a frenzy recounting a situation over and over in our heads to another person when we never had control of the outcome in the first place. Complaining also seems to help my damaged ego when I feel slighted by another person. It doesn't have to be another person; it can be a business. In this case, the airline I work for who left me — and two other flight attendants — stranded in an airport for six hours.

All this toxic texting with Trick Daddy did nothing but raise my heart rate, reinforce the hatred I had towards the airline industry, and leave me feeling as miserable as I was while sitting in the airport awaiting a hotel room.

When the taxi pulled under the hotel's porte-cochère, I sat in the front seat while the driver struggled with the credit card machine. I found that odd, but I was too sleepy to become agitated. Lana and Maria grabbed all of our bags from the trunk and waited on the curb for me to finish what should have been a smooth transaction.

"Please. Let me try." I insisted while taking the machine out of his hand and swiping my credit card a few times until the charge accepted. I speculated that he was stealing my identity, but I was too drained to care. I'd deal with it in the morning when I woke up and found out I had purchased a few sex slaves from India.

As we waited for our room keys, I received the email from Root confirming our airport shuttle pick up time was scheduled for 11:30 a.m.

After what seemed like a never-ending evening of waiting and being placed on hold, we finally stepped off the elevator and walked into our rooms at 3:15 a.m.

Or was it 3:30 a.m.? Honestly, it's all irrelevant after 2:00 a.m.

The hotel room was extravagant. Before taking off any of my clothes, I walked from the foyer — yes, I said foyer — to the bathroom and then into the bedroom while turning on every light fixture. My airline never puts us up in hotels as elegant as the one I was strutting through while kicking off my shoes and removing my tie. I take that back; the airline does put us up in a few lavish hotels, but nothing that resembles Mariah Carey's guest house. My aggression and demands paid off; I expected Crew Scheduling dished out at least $500 per room for the three of us to spend the night. The sad part was that we were staying less than eight hours behind the door. That made me grunt while undressing for bed. Here I was, in an incredible hotel room, a once in a decade opportunity in the airline industry, with barely enough time to test out the sheets.

I debated whether I wanted to take a pleasant bubble bath in the oversized tub. It was spectacular. Instead, I stuck with a regular nightcap masturbation session before shutting off my light and passing out. In hindsight that was probably the best decision. As exhausted as I was, I'd never have made it out of the tub alive. And we can't have that; I'm a Thomas, not a Houston.

The next morning, I fought to get out of the bed. I spent the better part of the morning tossing and turning and only clocked in about four hours sleep. Five hours if I was lucky. Even if our schedule went as planned, the day would drag on like a *Jersey Shore* marathon.

The three of us met in the hotel lobby and dragged ourselves out to the shuttle van like extras in *The Walking Dead*. I had zero confidence the shuttle driver would be there at 11:30 a.m., but I was pleasantly surprised to see him idled outside at 11:25 a.m.

The second we fastened our seat belts, the driver asked the three of us how we were, and I detonated like ISIS at a market in Raqqa.

I barely stopped to breathe while flinging around grievance after grievance. Most of the time, I made no sense and had Lana, Maria, and the driver laughing hysterically.

"How are we doing? Not good. Not good at all. We got fucked by our airline. Major fucking. Hardcore fucking with no lube. No condom, either. Who needs a condom when you're getting held down and ass raped? Prisoners don't get fucked that hard by their cellmates. They left us at the airport for six hours. Am I right?"

Lana and Maria chimed in between snorts and breaks between laughter to agree.

I continued with no signs of stopping, "I hope your company doesn't fuck you like that. If they do, I hope they're using lube so you can walk the next day. I could barely make it down the elevator because they fucked us so hard last night. No wonder I couldn't sleep. I'm trying to recover from six hours of anal."

It's not an exaggeration that I gripped the entire 20 minutes to the airport. As the driver pulled up at the departures level, I changed my demeanor and smiled. "Don't report me for any of that. I'll deny it."

The three of them howled, which made me realize my verbal explosion was safe inside the taxi.

The driver finally had a moment to speak, "Nah man, you're good. Funny."

I stepped into the airport secretly hoping he reported me. That's an easy ticket out of such a chaotic industry.

At the gate, the agent informed the three of us that Crew Scheduling had listed us positive space for the Orlando to Houston flight but had forgotten about the Houston to Los Angeles flight, and it was full.

Anxiety level breach in three, two, one.

Before I go any further, let me explain positive space travel. It is the airline's responsibility to transport flight attendants and pilots to their originating base whenever there is a schedule disruption. In this case, it was the three of us being canceled in Orlando and removed from the remainder of our trip. Positive space also comes in handy when airlines have to fly crew — or other airline employees — to their corporate headquarters for meetings and training classes. There is a myriad of reasons why airlines use positive space travel, but in my experience, the most common is flight recovery, in other words, moving flight attendants and pilots around from one airport to another to work flights missing the crew.

That explanation should trigger a memory in your brain from a dramatic situation that took place in April 2017, when a United Airlines passenger was aggressively, and brutally, dragged off an airplane because he refused to follow direction from the airline employees and give up his seat on a full flight. Now, I am not here to debate whether the passenger was right or the airline was wrong.

However, I will state this; I have no sympathy for a person who doesn't respect themselves enough to walk off an airplane on their own two feet. Unless, of course, they don't have two feet. I guess if they were footless, dragging would be acceptable.

No. There's always the wheelchair option. I have gotten way off topic; I guess what I am saying is there are exceptions. But, if you do have two working feet, your ass better stand up and walk off the airplane. When this happened, I tried putting myself in that predicament. I said, "Self, what would you do if faced with being asked to give up your seat on an airplane after paying for a ticket?"

I'd be furious. I'd curse. I'd scream. I'd probably throw my carry-on bag around while I pulled it out from the overhead bin and threatened to sue until the name Flight Attendant Joe was painted on every airplane the airline owned. What I wouldn't do, and I can promise this, is get dragged out like some untamed animal by the police.

There are undoubtedly ways this situation could have ended on a happier note, although the estimated settlement the passenger received was north of a million dollars. That sounds pretty happy to me. But seriously, do I know the answer on how to prevent these types of events in the future? Hell no. I serve nuts and cans of Dr. Pepper to fat ladies in coach; I don't solve airline problems. I do know that United Airlines followed protocol and when the passenger refused to get up, they contacted the Department of Transportation (DOT). When the passenger refused to listen to the DOT, they yanked him off the airplane.

Why did this even happen? United had to transport four crew to Louisville to work a flight to prevent it from canceling and leaving passengers stranded. You have to ask yourself, looking at the big picture, whether it is better to have one person stranded or hundreds? Airlines will always have to transport crew from one airport to another. It's hard not to believe that anyone sitting in the airport in Louisville, waiting on the crew to arrive to fly them off to their destination, would not personally pull off one airline passenger holding everyone else up.

"What should we do in Houston?" I asked the gate agent. I began to panic, but Lana and Maria were still too exhausted to care.

The gate agent brushed off my concern, "I have no clue. Talk to them when you get to Houston."

On our way to Houston, I spent the entire flight writing an email to the director of our department. I copied in as many people as I could: managers, supervisors, pilots, flight attendants, janitors... if I knew them, they were copied in on the email. The only reason Jesus Christ wasn't on the list was that I had no faith he'd respond. Listen, he hasn't made an appearance in 2,000 years; I doubt he's going to care about my work grievance.

As expected, I eventually received a mediocre response to my email. Unsurprisingly, there was no indication that Root would be held accountable for his negligence.

The flight landed, and while I stayed behind to help clean the airplane for the next flight, Lana ran up to the gate to get our seat assignments. The gate agent welcomed her with a gruff, "They don't have you listed, and the flight is full."

After about 10 minutes, I walked up the jet bridge to survey the crisis at the gate. At my airline, if it takes longer than five minutes to solve an issue, it's a fucking crisis.

Lana was still talking with the gate agent when I stepped beside her, "What's the problem?" I promise that my nasty attitude shined brighter than a full moon.

"They still don't have you listed for the flight," the enthusiastic gate agent announced, "I don't know what you're gonna do."

Did he want to see who could be a bitchier queen? Was it a contest? He was in for an education and lesson, "What we're going to do is get three seats on the flight."

We stared at each other for a few moments and then he threw his hands up, "Sarah, please come deal with this. I need to start boarding."

Sarah walked over and maintained a slightly higher level of professionalism, "Can you guys take the jumpseat?"

"We can, but we don't have to. We had a very short layover last night, and I'm not taking the chance at falling asleep on the jumpseat and being terminated." I looked at Lana, "Are you?"

She shook her head. "No. We need our seats."

The three of us stared at each for a few seconds, and then the captain walked up to the gate and stepped into the conversation, "What's going on? The deadheading flight attendant down there said you guys hadn't received your seats yet."

Sarah jumped in, "It looks like they have finally listed you, but the flight is full. Now we are oversold. And we are going to have to pull passengers off the flight."

The captain looked at her and shrugged, "Okay. Then that's what we do. We're responsible for getting flight attendants back to base in a passenger seat."

"This will cause a delay." Sarah pushed back to the captain.

He was not playing with her, "How many passengers haven't checked in?"

She tapped away at the computer, "Eight."

"Give them three seats," he rolled his eyes, "boarding is almost complete. Obviously, those passengers are not making this flight." Without another word, he turned around and walked away towards the jet bridge.

Sarah handed us our boarding passes, and we made our way onto the airplane and found our seats. I was in a window, Maria was in an aisle seat, and Lana was in the middle somewhere in the back of the airplane.

We were all in seats and on our way back to Los Angeles, nothing else mattered, including the broken television I stared at for the three-hour flight.

The Santa Hat

During flight attendant interviews, management informs the eager candidates that they will have to work on holidays. There's no ambiguity, no room for interpretation. When you are a junior flight attendant, you will work these days. No ifs, ands, or big butts about it.

The management representative stands in the middle of the hotel conference room and announces, "You will not be home for Christmas. You will not be home on Thanksgiving. You might be in Miami on New Year's Eve and most likely Dallas on Easter. If your birthday falls on a weekend, you'll be spending it with strangers at 38,000 feet."

They leave out Ramadan and Yom Kippur, but my best guess is you won't be home for those holidays either.

Want to watch fireworks on the 4th of July? You'll be watching them from the window at your jumpseat while you land in Newark. Care about sinking your teeth into some turkey on Thanksgiving? You'll have to make due with a tomato, wilted lettuce, and turkey sandwich from the airport that cost $13.00 after your employee discount.

During the interview process and training, flight attendants will agree to almost anything.

Interviewer, "You won't be home for Christmas."

Future flight attendant, "That's fine. I want this job more than anything."

"You will most likely not be celebrating your birthday with loved ones."

"I'm cool with that. Who wants to turn another year older?"

"You might not be maid of honor in your sister's wedding."

"Thank goodness; I don't like her fiancé anyway."

The shock of seeing your initial schedule slaps you like two titties during an intense motorboat session.

When you get your first schedule, those events you didn't care about missing during your interview and six weeks of training become the most critical items on your calendar.

I can't begin to recall all the times I've overheard newbie flight attendant conversations where one of them will state, "I can't work that weekend, so I'm just going to talk to my supervisor and have him take me off the schedule."

I imagine their heads explode when they sit down at the supervisor's desk and don't hear the answers they expected.

Newbie flight attendant in November, "I didn't know I'd have to work Christmas. My family always gets together for Christmas. I simply can't miss it."

Supervisor, "We told you during flight attendant training that you probably wouldn't be home for Christmas."

Newbie flight attendant in March, "How do you expect me not to celebrate my birthday with my fiance?"

Supervisor, "We told you during flight attendant training you wouldn't be celebrating your birthday with loved ones."

Newbie flight attendant in June, "I can't work that weekend. I'm the maid of honor in my sister's wedding."

Supervisor, "We told you during flight attendant training you'd probably miss most important celebrations."

That's the moment I expect heads to explode. But don't think that's going to get you out of your assigned trip, a blown apart head is still no reason to call in sick.

Once flight attendants graduate from training and realize that management meant it when they said we'd be working weekends, holidays, and every significant occasion they start calling in sick. And boy do they call in sick. Flight attendants love to call in sick (myself included). During my first six months, I called in enough to be put on disciplinary action. After that, I learned my lesson and realized calling in sick for a hangnail was probably not good for my flight attendant career.

Managing sick calls in the airline industry is extremely challenging. Flights cancel because of flight attendants calling in sick. Don't get me wrong; if you are genuinely ill, you should call in. But there are times when flight attendants call in sick because they received Lady Gaga tickets at the last minute and NOBODY MISSES GAGA!

A few abuse the system, but there are times when we are legitimately sick, and the airline doesn't help the situation by scheduling us to work 10, 11, or even 12 days in a row during the holiday season. We are only human, but to the airline executives, we are machines, expected to continue operating at all costs. That might be a slight exaggeration, but that's how it feels. I understand the airline needs me, and I appreciate that, but if they want flight attendants not to work themselves sick, they shouldn't give them schedules that would make child laborers strike.

Calling in sick during the holidays is serious. It's like saying you don't care about anyone but yourself, even if you are coughing up green mucus and can't move due to a high fever. During the holidays, flight attendants receive monetary incentives for not calling in sick. That means many of the flight attendants on your flights probably have something you could take home to your baby. I have a pilot friend who refuses to fly with flight attendants and pilots who are sick. I don't blame him.

I try and give back to the airline and my coworkers during the holidays. Now that I am senior enough to hold off weekends, holidays, and my birthday — I choose to work on Christmas. It's the holiday that I usually schedule myself to work. Why? First off, I am not a Christian, so why would I need to take it off? I don't take off Jewish holidays or Muslim holidays. My holiday is the third Thursday in November. I never work on Thanksgiving. If I am going to worship anything, it's food, and if you don't believe me, just check my 36-inch waistline. I am a food zealot. Second, I like to give coworkers with less seniority a chance to be home with their children. I've worked almost every Christmas since becoming a flight attendant, so I figure that's at least one flight attendant per year who has received Christmas off because of me. That's some decent karma I am putting out there in the world. Hopefully, it will come back to me if I ever forget to bid and screw up my schedule.

I guarantee you that's not how karma works in the airline industry. There's only one type of karma in the airline industry, and that's the kind that feels like a steel pole inserted into your rectum. Fun for some flight attendants, but not for us who like to walk to the mailbox to collect our Amazon packages.

Another great reason to work on Christmas is the marvelous trips left in open time to pick up. Most senior flight attendants, I can't speak for all — only most — don't give a fuck about junior flight attendants. Because of that, they bid Christmas off, which leaves a sea of incredible trips with unbelievable layovers waiting to be scooped up. A trip I'd never hold if it wasn't during a holiday. A nice Aruba layover, an extended San Juan, or — if I'm fortunate — a remarkably long Honolulu layover.

A few years ago, while based in LAX, I was awarded a 24-hour layover in Turks and Caicos on Christmas. That was like receiving a present fit for a Kardashian. I had been to Turks and Caicos on a short 12-hour layover in the past, but never long enough to have fun. The hotel was on the other side of the island — far from the airport — so by the time we landed, made our way through Customs, rode in the van to the hotel, it was time for bed.

On Christmas Eve and Christmas Day I wear a Santa hat with my uniform. You'd be surprised by the amount of joy a flight attendant wearing a Santa hat brings to passengers traveling during the holidays. I don't just consider Christians; my Santa hat is blue and white for the Jews. I cover my bases, especially if I happen to be working a flight to South Florida.

We all know that Christmas is stressful. The shopping. The traffic. The credit card debt. With all that aggravation, it disappoints me that people have found an additional way to make the holiday even more fucking annoying.

And they found it in two simple words.

Have you seen the way some Christians react to being greeted with, "Happy Holidays." It's ridiculous how insulted and offended the God-fearing get over not hearing the two words, Merry Christmas. Personally, I don't care how someone greets me during the holidays. They can wish me a Happy Kwanzaa, and I'd be thrilled. In this day and age, with how rude and disrespectful people are towards each other, I think any endearing sentiment will impress me. Take the time to address me and wish me well; I'll respond back however you want.

That's why I stick with Happy Holidays on the airplane. It's easy, and I don't have to think about it. I barely remember drink orders on the aircraft, trying to assume what holiday passengers celebrate will only cause a brain bleed. If a passenger wants to reciprocate with a friendly, "Merry Christmas," or, "Happy Hanukkah," as they walk off the airplane, then so be it.

During December it usually goes like this as passengers deplane:

Me, "Happy Holidays."

California female passenger, "Happy Holidays."

Me, "Happy Holidays."

The man from Raleigh, "It's Merry Christmas."

Me, "Yup. That too."

The airline pays me to be polite. A passenger could wish me a Happy 9/11, and I'd probably return the gesture. On second thought, I'd call security. Anyone who says Happy 9/11 is most likely a threat to the aircraft.

For my Turks and Caicos layover, I commuted to LAX and met the two flight attendants working the three day trip with me. Theresa Batista was the senior flight attendant and the lead on the flight. I had heard about Theresa through word of mouth but had never flown with her. Jan Buster, who I had never heard of or met before, was the mid-cabin flight attendant, which left me working the back galley. Theresa and I both sported Santa hats, and Jan was envious.

She brought it up while we completed our crew briefing, "I feel left out. I want a hat."

I adjusted my hat and responded, "Sorry, I just have this one."

Theresa's enthusiasm seeped out, "Hold on," she reached into her bag and pulled out a plastic bag, "here, honey, you can use this one. Be careful though; it means a lot to me."

Jan slapped it on her head and moved around like a queen who just received her crown, "How's this look? Now we all match."

"You look fantastic," Theresa echoed as she slung her tote bag over her shoulder and walked out of the lounge with us following behind like two adoring fans. We strolled through the airport, with our Santa hats flopping around, like the Three Kings who brought gifts to the newborn baby Jesus. But we were not the Three Kings, we were just the Three Flight Attendants bringing bags of salty nuts to passengers heading to JFK.

Our trip consisted of one flight to JFK, with a short overnight layover, and then one flight to Turks and Caicos on Christmas Eve for a 24-hour layover. My excitement to spend the Christmas holiday on the island of Turks and

Caicos had me bouncing off the walls in the back galley while we completed our security checks.

With a handful of lavatory napkins, I stuffed them into my blue Santa hat, so it stood straight up on my head, "Jan, look… my hat has a hard-on."

Laughing, "Joe, that's ridiculous. Wear it like that throughout the flight."

"Is that a dare? Done."

Because I was in the back of the airplane, I barely had any interaction with the passengers during boarding. Only a few using the back galley lavatory had the chance to share their comments about our silly hats. Mine, blue of course, Theresa's red, and Jan's a hodgepodge of decorations.

Anyone working with Theresa realized that when she was the lead flight attendant, the passengers did not need any other flight attendant interaction. She instantly overflowed the passenger interaction cup. Before I go any further, I want to clarify that I enjoyed Theresa immensely. Yes, she drove me fucking nuts, but she came from a genuinely joyous place. Quirky, over-friendly, and loved to talk about herself.

She was practically the female version of me, except for one huge difference, (No, not that she had a vagina. Although that's a huge difference, too) Theresa was a celebrator.

In my book, *Fasten Your Seat Belts And Eat Your Fucking Nuts*, I spelled out the various flight attendant "types" I had encountered throughout the years. When I wrote the definition for The Celebrator, it was in honor of Theresa.

The Celebrator: *Keeps so busy celebrating passengers' birthdays, anniversaries, engagements, bar mitzvahs, first time*

---

periods, and sex reassignment surgeries that she has no time to do the job she's actually paid to fucking do.

That was Theresa. A full-time celebrator. It didn't matter how stressed the boarding was, how demanding the passengers were, or how unhappy the entire airplane felt, Theresa was prepared to force everyone into a great mood. Or piss them off. More often, when it came to the flight attendants she worked with, it was the latter.

It started innocently enough over the PA after the safety demonstration, "Do we have any first-time flyers?"

That was fine, I guess.

Then came the more aggressive questioning. Is anyone celebrating an anniversary? An engagement? A divorce? Gender reassignment surgery?

My ears practically bled in the back galley from her announcements, but I kept my mouth shut and prayed to my Santa hat that she'd shut the fuck up.

She didn't.

"Are any of you celebrating a birthday anytime soon?"

That's when the hands went up. I didn't bother counting because I was too busy stuffing extra napkins inside my hat for a fully erect effect.

As if triggered by an orgasm, she became giddy with delight, "Oh wonderful! I have a birthday song for you." Then she broadcasted for all of us, "Happy Birthday to you/Happy Birthday to you/I haven't gotten any more for you/So that's your song." And then she immediately placed the interphone back in its holder.

Everyone erupted into applause; I shook my head in amazement. The idea of blowing the emergency slide and escaping so not to endure all her nonsense for three days ran through my mind. Who the fuck wants to be held prisoner for days on end listening to that bullshit? In the end, I strapped myself into my jumpseat and prayed that this was a one-off event.

The next morning in JFK, our boarding was incredibly stressful. The captain came out during boarding and announced there'd be turbulence on our way to Turks and Caicos. That's all the lady in 3A needed to hear before becoming unhinged.

And I mean unhinged.

She rang her call bell, and Jan approached the row, "May I help you?"

"Is it true there's gonna be turbulence on this flight?"

"I believe that's what the captain said. There are storms along the east coast. Nothing to worry about."

"Oh, that's not gonna work for me."

She was traveling with her husband, two sons, and teenage daughter. Her husband and daughter sat across the row from her and the boys. Before Jan had the chance to calm the situation, the woman turned quickly to her sons, "There's gonna be turbulence. If you don't wanna go on this trip, you just tell me."

You heard that right. Without discussing with her husband, she relinquished all the family power to her twin seven-year-old sons. Thousands of dollars spent on a vacation in the hands of two bratty fucking kids.

They instantly turned into newborns, "No. we don't wanna go, mommy."

The lady threw her hands in the air and called foul on the entire flight. At no time during the incident did she discuss the situation with her husband. It was as if she was traveling alone with her sons. Ridiculous as it sounds, it made perfect sense why her husband and daughter sat on the other side of the airplane like complete strangers. If I were that guy, I'd have been texting my divorce lawyer the moment she stood up and generated bedlam.

Boarding halted, and Theresa contacted the gate agent to accommodate Mrs. Wacko and her two sons, who had not fallen far from the Wacko family tree. During the kerfuffle, the captain overheard the ruckus and came out of the flight deck.

He approached Mrs. Wacko standing in the galley awaiting the gate agent. "What's the problem?"

She stood her ground, "You told us there'd be turbulence and my sons are scared."

"Yes. There will be slight turbulence, but it's nothing to worry about it."

"That's easy for you to say," she pulled her bags closer to her, "We'll take a flight tomorrow and meet the rest of our family there."

The captain chuckled, 'There's gonna be turbulence tomorrow, also. There are storms along the east coast."

She didn't like that. "We'll take our chances tomorrow."

Without another word, the captain strolled back into the flight deck. The boarding process resumed, and a few minutes later the gate agent arrived and escorted them off the airplane leaving behind the husband and teenage daughter to fly to Turks and Caicos. I'd never experienced anything like that in my entire life. It was bizarre, but after dealing with Mrs. Wacko for five minutes, I can only guess that her husband and daughter were thrilled about having a quiet and calm Christmas Eve.

I still feel bad for those twin boys.

After regaining order of the boarding process, we closed the airplane door and conducted our safety demonstration.

International flights require a documentation bag "doc bag" that holds all the necessary paperwork needed to enter the foreign country. The lead flight attendant is in charge of keeping track of the doc bag and also making sure that all the correct forms are available. There's nothing like standing up in the galley, at 38,000 feet, on your way to Haiti and discovering you don't have the necessary customs forms to hand out to the passengers. That type of panic needs to be resolved by a defibrillator to the heart.

Because I like to fill out my paperwork promptly, I walked up to the front galley, pulled the doc bag from the overhead bin, and began rummaging through looking for a customs form.

Theresa walked over to me, "What are you looking for?"

"Where's the crew form we have to fill out?"

"What form?

"The form we always fill out when we land in another country."

She frowned, "We don't have to fill out any paperwork."

I rebutted, "Of course we do. We're going to a foreign country."

"No. I was just there last month. We didn't have to fill out any paperwork?"

I stared at her. There was no doubt in my mind that I was accurate regarding the paperwork, but then I started doubting myself. Has that ever happened to you? You go into a discussion convinced you are correct, but the person you are debating is especially adamant and confident in their delivery, making you question yourself?

That's the story of my life. I looked at Jan, "You know what I'm talking about, right?"

Jan shrugged, "I never work on these flights. I couldn't tell ya."

As confident as a politician, Theresa continued, "Yeah. I never fill out paperwork on this flight," she picked up the interphone and went straight into her celebratory dance. I walked to the back of the airplane and pulled out my flight attendant manual to confirm that I wasn't the crazy one.

On the flight to Turks and Caicos, we had multiple birthdays. Three to be exact. I had no idea how this affected me until we departed and Theresa came to the back galley with cards, air sickness bags, and candy. Carefully, she wrote out cards, filled air sickness bags with candy, and turned plastic gloves into balloons.

"Okay, Joe, what do you want to do?"

"I want you to read this, right here," I pointed in my manual, "when we land we fill out this form."

She got defensive, "Joe, I was just there last month, and we did not have to fill out any paperwork. Maybe they haven't updated the manual. I don't know, all I know is what I did and did not do."

I refused to let it go, "It's right here in black and white. This form is what we have to fill out. I'm telling you." I pointed hard at the manual while she continued folding air sickness bags.

"It will be fine, Joe. Now, what do you want to do for birthdays?"

Was Theresa related to Mrs. Wacko? Was Theresa, Grandma Wacko? Were we starring in an episode of *The*

Twilight Zone? It seemed possible, especially while standing there providing her with facts and all she cared about was blowing up five finger gloved balloons. I slowly closed my manual and placed it back in my tote bag. Once I put my manual away, I told myself to stop worrying about it. Fuck it. She was the lead flight attendant, let her deal with it. If an agent stopped us at customs, I'd just point all my fingers at her and watch as they carried her off to a Turks and Caicos prison, which I can't lie, sounded fabulous.

My daydreaming abruptly stopped, "Joe? What do you want to do?"

I snapped back into her conversation, "Excuse me? Do what for what?"

"We're gonna go out and sing happy birthday to these passengers. Do you want to carry the balloons, the bag of candy, or the paper candle?"

It was worse than *The Twilight Zone*; it was like being trapped at the Bates Motel, "Paper candle?"

She produced a fake construction paper candle from her bag and began to mimic how to work it, "Yes. You pull this piece of paper first, then they blow out the candle, and then you tug on this."

I was fucking lost. I take that back; I knew where I was, Theresa was just fucking delusional. All I wanted to do was drink on a marvelous island and enjoy my holiday, not play happy birthday with adults. What was next? Dungeons and Dragons.

"I don't think I want to do that. I'll just stay back here and serve any passengers who need something."

"Don't be silly, Joe. We're all gonna go out there," she looked over at Jan who sat on the jumpseat wearing her borrowed Santa hat ignoring the conversation happening a few feet away. She may have thought she was sneaky, but there was no way I'd be forced to participate in this fiasco while she sat on the jumpseat twiddling her fingers.

Jan gingerly sputtered out,"I guess I'll carry the balloons."

"Wonderful. Joe, do you want to do the candle or the birthday bag?"

Fuck! My first thought was, if I were a Christian, I'd be home praying to Jesus. Which at that exact moment, sounded better than carrying vomit bags filled with candy through the airplane.

"I'll carry the candy bag. I'm not messing with that candle… thing." I folded. I'm weak and too helpful. Also, I blamed my Santa hat.

"Fantastic. Here, sign the card, and we'll go out before we start service."

A few seconds later the three of us marched through the aisle like toy soldiers. It was almost as embarrassing as shitting yourself at a bar. As you well know, I speak from experience on that subject.

Three passengers were celebrating their birthdays, and I barely managed singing and delivering barf bags filled with candy to two of them. Once I handed the third passenger their candy, I walked away as Jan and Theresa finished singing happy birthday, for the third time. At this rate, we'd be landing before service started. Jan wrapped up her mock *The Voice* audition and hastened to the back galley. Even though Jan didn't speak a negative word towards Theresa, I sensed she was over the enthusiastic bullshit.

We landed on time, collected our belongings, and follow the passengers off the airplane. The three of us made

194

our way through the airport towards the crew custom lanes when Theresa stopped me, "I'm going to let this family come through the customs line with us. I'm gonna tell customs they are my family."

Puzzled I asked, 'You're going to do what? You can't do that."

"I feel bad for the family. They're so nice and were in my section. I told them I'd get them through faster so they wouldn't have to wait."

I stared at her as if her Santa hat came to life. "I don't feel comfortable with this. You do what you want, but I'm not involved."

"Nothing will happen. I'm going to say they're with me. I just feel so bad."

Why she felt sorry for them, I have no clue, and I didn't ask. I stayed a few feet behind Jan as she walked between us. I looked around to keep an eye on the police. When they started handcuffing and throwing flight attendants around, I wanted no part in it.

Theresa stepped up to the counter and spoke with the customs agent. I have no clue what was said, all I can tell you is that the woman behind the counter meant business. The agent's scowl was a reminder that she didn't give a damn who you were, what airline you worked for, or who the fuck your family happened to be. It was Christmas Eve, and the custom and immigration lines snaked around the entire building. This agent would be lucky to get home before Santa snuck down the chimney. I stood there waiting for the shit to hit the fan.

Jan turned and placed her hand on her head, "I left the Santa hat on the airplane."

Theresa stood about 10 feet away, but the moment she heard, "…Santa hat on the airplane," she spun around and focused on Jan. She quickly forgot about her "family" going through the crew line and took a step towards us, "Where's that Santa hat?"

"I left it on the airplane."

Theresa scurried over to us in line, "You did what? How could you do that?'

"It was an accident. I took it off because my head was sweating. I think I put it on the jumpseat."

"You think? Did you or didn't you? We have to get that hat back." Theresa's voice rose as she spoke and I waited for her to start shaking Jan uncontrollably. Thankfully, she didn't. She moved swiftly back to the counter and leaned over it towards the agent, "We left something on the airplane, can we go get it."

Like I said already, the agent didn't give a damn about us. "We will get someone for you in a minute. Do you have your passport?"

"Did you hear me? We have to get back on the airplane." She became aggressive while placing her passport on the counter for the agent. I considered what life would be like in a Turks and Caicos prison. At first, I thought it would be fantastic, but after seeing the attitude on these customs agents, I expected to be hungry a lot and have AIDS by the end of the year. And let's not forget, it was already December 24.

Jan spoke up, "I'll run over to the gate doors and see if they can help me. Joe, can you watch my bags?"

"Yeah. Be careful." I stood there holding our bags while Theresa paced back and forth.

"How could she be so careless? I lent her that hat. Who just leaves something on the airplane that someone lets them borrow?"

I didn't know what to say. All I wanted was to get to the hotel so I could start my layover, "It was an accident. Jan will get the hat back.

Theresa's eyes began to water. It was puzzling. What did she have in that hat? Her life savings? Did I even care?

The customs agent was over Theresa's dramatics as she held her passport in her hand, "We need to process you. Where's your paperwork?"

She stopped pacing and looked at her cross-eyed, "Paperwork? What paperwork?"

The prison idea started becoming more of certainty. There was also no sign of Jan. I expected she'd already been scooped up, sold into prostitution, and on a ship headed for Miami. Now I'd be stuck with her bags for eternity.

"Yes. You must fill out paperwork." The agent sternly said.

"No, we don't. I was just here last month, and we didn't have to fill out paperwork."

"You most certainly did. You can not come into this country without the proper paperwork. Flight crew or not."

Theresa wouldn't let up, "I specifically remember that we just walked through." She looked over at me, but I stared at my watch wishing it had a time travel feature.

After she wasted two more minutes arguing with the agent, I felt it was time to step in, "Theresa, it doesn't matter. Just fill out the paperwork. It takes a few minutes." I walked up to the counter and pulled out my pen while addressing the agent, "Do you have a form?"

The agent handed me three forms as Jan ran up to the counter, "They wouldn't let me down the jet bridge. There's nobody there to let me back on the airplane."

I handed her a form, "Here. You've got to fill this out."

"I thought we didn't have to fill out any forms."

Directing my eyes at her, I rolled them hard while finding a place on the counter to fill out my form. I was first to finish and quickly nudged Theresa out of the way and handed the paperwork to the agent. She stamped the piece of paper, and I walked through the turn stall and into Turks and Caicos. Sadly, there was no frozen drink in my hand, but happy there were no police cuffs, either.

Jan followed next while Theresa continued debating with the agent about the need to fill out paperwork. I tapped my finger on my arm waiting for her to finish. I fought the urge to tell her to shut the fuck up. It was on the tip of my tongue; I am still shocked it never came spewing out.

Her mania intensified the second she walked through the turn stall. "We have to get back on that airplane and get that hat. I can't believe this is happening."

I agreed, I too couldn't believe any of this was happening on my Christmas Eve layover. We followed her through the terminal and out into the busy, chaotic scene outside the airport. The second we stepped outside a woman approached us, "Yes. Please follow me this way."

I had no clue who she was, but I instantly followed her. Who accompanies a stranger in a strange land? Shocked I was never abducted as a child. All some unknown man had to do was show me an orange creamsicle popsicle, and I'd have been found months later in his closet.

We didn't get far before Theresa jumped in, "Excuse me? How do I get to the ticket counter? I need to get something off the airplane."

The woman pointed towards a building separated from the rest of the airport, "Over there. That's where you want to go. Would you like us to wait for you?"

"Well of course. I don't know where I'm going," Theresa answered frustrated. She had no clue I was the one truly frustrated. "Joe, can you please take my bags with you to the van? I will be right back."

I had no choice. I grabbed the handle of my bag and started dragging it behind me as I seized hers in the other hand. Without exaggerating, her suitcase was the most cumbersome bag I've ever pulled in my entire life. The only thing heavier would have been dragging a suitcase around with bricks packed inside. And the verdict wasn't out that her bag was, in fact, filled with bricks. My back started hurting. I wondered how it would look if I went out on an on-the-job injury because I was pulling a bag behind me that would have Hulk Hogan struggling. I watched Theresa disappear into the terminal, and I can't lie, I silently hoped that section of the airport fell into the ocean.

It didn't.

About 10 minutes after Jan and I boarded the hotel van, Theresa came running onto it. She was out of breath and sweating. She also had tears in her eyes. "They're trying to find someone to bring me down to the airplane."

I turned towards her and questioned,"What? You didn't get the hat?" I become irate, "Can't the other crew get it for you and leave it in the lounge? Why is this so difficult?"

"I don't know. Security won't let anyone go down to the aircraft."

My frustration was hard to hide, "This is ridiculous." I was also annoyed because this island was one of the only countries not on my free international texting and internet list. Not only was I trapped inside the van waiting for that magical fucking Santa hat, I was cut off from any rational human beings who would talk me out of slapping the shit out of Theresa before we got to the hotel.

Jan added, "I'm so sorry I left the hat on the airplane."

"You don't understand how important that hat is to me. It belonged to a friend of mine who died."

That caught my attention. Before I could respond, Jan jumped in, "Why would you lend it to me then? That's a lot of responsibility?"

"I didn't think you'd leave it on the airplane."

I added my ten cents worth, "Well, next time don't give out your precious keepsakes to a complete stranger."

By this time, the tears were flowing. I started questioning if the hat belonged to her friend or if it was the friend. Not that Theresa was crazy, but maybe she thought the Santa hat held the spirit of her dead friend.

Alright, I started believing she was crazy.

She got up from her seat, "I'm going back inside to see if they found anything.

By this time, 20 minutes had passed since we walked outside. It was the end of December, but I was sweating through my uniform. I was beyond frustrated and could barely speak. I sat there, staring at all the airline passengers jumping into their taxis, rental cars, and hugging family and friends, and here I was waiting for a fucking Santa hat. A Santa hat? Not even Santa, just his hat.

Jan continued beating herself up over the mishap, "I feel so bad that I left behind her hat."

I was pissed off, "Do you know what would happen if we had pilots with us? They'd fucking leave her behind. Figure your hat out on someone else's time."

"I know, right? Who lends something that personal to someone."

"Listen, some passengers have left behind their loved ones' ashes, and they weren't as upset as she is over that hat."

The driver stuck her head inside, "Do you know how much longer?"

Jan answered, "I don't know. I'm sorry. She had to run back onto the airplane and get something that was left behind." The driver nodded and stepped back out onto the curb. Jan turned back to me, "Do you want to get something to eat with us tonight."

"I don't want to be rude, but I won't be hanging out with you guys on this trip. Especially after all this drama."

Theresa enthusiastically stepped into the van with dried mascara on her face and a Santa hat in her hand. She addressed the driver, "Thank you for waiting. We're ready to go."

"Are you sure?" I couldn't hide my bitterness that we wasted over 30 minutes at the airport. I couldn't tell who I was angrier at — Jan or Theresa? My focus was on Theresa, but I also wasn't happy with Jan being careless. Stupid fucking Santa hat.

I kept my promise and spent the day alone. I enjoyed frozen cocktails and hung out among all the cruise ship patrons at a few local bars. When it was time to wrap up the evening, I made my way back to the hotel and found Theresa and Jan sitting at the bar having drinks. They waved me over, and so I didn't come off as a complete dickhead, I walked over.

Short and to the point, I listed off what I had accomplished on my layover — drinking and more drinking — and that I was ready to call it a night and go to sleep. They invited me to have a drink with them, but I declined.

The next morning I stepped out of the shower and heard a knock at the door. I walked over to the door thinking it was housekeeping. Through the door, I answered, "Hello?"

"Joe. It's me, Theresa. I wanted to give you a big giant Christmas hug."

Was she serious? I peered through the peephole — she was serious, "I'm naked right now, so that's not the best idea."

"I'm going to slip this card under your door. I'll be getting something to eat downstairs before our van time. See you then."

She slipped a card under the door and disappeared. I felt terrible. My frustration with her from the previous night finally started to vanish. Sure, she was quirky, odd, and melodramatic about a piece of stitched felt — but it was imperative to her to collect it off the airplane. Would I want someone to be patient with me if the same situation occurred regarding something near and dear to my heart? Of course. But I wouldn't lend it to a complete stranger. I don't even lend out pens on the airplane.

After getting dressed, I made my way downstairs and missed breakfast. The restaurant was closing as I walked in.

Theresa offered to share her muffin with me, but because I felt guilty about my behavior the day before, I declined. You can not act like an asshole towards a person and then eat their muffin. On second thought, I probably should have taken it as payment for stealing 30 minutes of my layover. It was only half a muffin, so it wasn't full payment, but it was a start.

Jan stepped into the lobby, and Theresa stood up first, "I need to cash out my bill at the front desk."

"Cool. I'll go see if the van is here."

We walked into the lobby and I noticed the checkout line was very long. Theresa was seventh in line, and Jan was number five. I frowned realizing this would put us behind schedule. Our van time was 11:00 a.m. and my watch read 10:57 a.m.

I stepped outside into the humid morning air and smiled at the male driver waiting beside the van with the back doors open for our luggage. I pulled my bags over to him, "The other two flight attendants will be out in a few minutes."

At 11:17 a.m., I was mad again. The driver asked, "Do you know where they are? I'm scheduled to pick someone else up on the way. This delay is making us late." We were now 17 minutes behind schedule to leave for the airport. I hate being tardy. My temper rose as I found myself sitting in a hotel van waiting on Theresa for the second time in my life.

"They should be out at any moment," I was guessing, "We can stop on the way and pick up the other passenger. I'm sorry about this."

He shrugged his shoulders and walked back to the front of the van. As they strolled out of the hotel and made their way towards us, I could feel my blood pressure in the air. My frustration was palpable. They sauntered into the van and took their seats. I gazed out the window so as not to say something that would get me fired.

It's one thing to wait around because someone is searching for something on the airplane — and that's even pushing it — but waiting almost 20 minutes because they had charges sent to their room and didn't calculate the time it took to check out and leave on time made me livid.

The driver pulled the door closed, climbed into his seat, and announced, "I have to make an additional stop to pick someone else up on the way to the airport."

Theresa interrupted, "What? We need to go to the airport. We're already running behind schedule."

I couldn't take it anymore. I did a Mount St. Helens in the van, "We're running late because of you. Van time was 11:00 a.m., and it's 11:20 a.m. If we're late at the gate, it's because of you. Not the driver."

During the ride, we sat in silence. It was welcoming. I enjoyed it. No crying about a fucking Santa hat. No talk about being late. No discussion about anything.

At the airport, our airplane had not yet landed. There were no worries about being reprimanded for arriving at the gate late. That was reassuring. There was still a sense of unease among the three of us. I stood at the side of the gate awaiting the arrival of the airplane while attempting to control my hangry demeanor — yes, hangry — that had been ignited by annoyance with Theresa and not having breakfast.

The airplane arrived, and after we boarded up our 16 passengers, people don't fly much on Christmas, we departed for JFK. Even with 16 passengers on the airplane, the moment we got to 10,000 feet, Theresa was on the interphone asking if there were any birthdays, first-time flyers, or anniversaries.

When it came time to help hand out the air sickness bags filled with candy, I declined.

Nobody questioned me.

Journal Entry:
Seniority Rules

Dear Journal,

I'm working with a flight attendant who I do not like. Before you judge me, I've already shared that I dislike most people, so this should come as no shock. In my defense, this lady deserves my dislike, and that happened before I ever set foot on an airplane with her.

First impressions are important to me. I usually form an opinion about someone within the first few minutes of interaction. I'm sure people do the same with me, and that's probably why many people don't like me. I guess I deserve that.

But this lady is different. My brain can't like her. She could buy me Starbucks for a week, and my feelings would not change. I'd drink the coffee, but I'd still resent her.

Before working with Shelley, we had two interactions which left a nasty taste in my mouth the moment I saw her name on my pairing.

Shelley is all about seniority. And I agree, seniority is crucial. It's the only reason flight attendants stay in this business for so long. Seniority defines our schedules, days off, base transfers — everything. But Shelley takes her obsession with seniority to an entirely different level.

When I met Shelley, I had recently transferred to LAX from Cleveland and didn't know many of the local flight attendants. I sat in the kitchen area of the flight attendant lounge, working on my book, when she walked in and started making herself a cup of coffee. I noticed her eyeing me like a cake donut left out on the counter, but I ignored her.

While I tapped away at my laptop, she aggressively waved at me. I caught her out of the corner of my eye and removed my earbuds to hear her gruffly ask, "Who are you? I don't know you."

It took me by surprise. I had no clue Shelley was the mayor of the flight attendant lounge, "I'm Joe."

"I'm Shelley. Yeah, I don't know you. When did you transfer here?"

As I said, it caught me off guard, but I wasn't annoyed… yet. Behavior like that is typical in a smaller, more senior base. And our LAX base is our most senior base in the entire airline. In LAX, everyone knows everything about everyone. There are no secrets. I wait for the day that I shitstorm in the lounge restroom and by the time I flush, there's a memo sent out to the base regarding my stinky ass. It's that bad.

Not my ass, but the small base.

Okay, my ass is terrible, too.

"I transferred last month." I decided playing along was my best bet. I had no idea who she was, either. Maybe she was the mayor? If so, they ran things differently in LA.

"How long have you been here?"

I answered still smiling, "A month."

"You've been with the airline for a month?"

"No!" Was she fucking kidding me? "I've been here for seven years."

Her pleasantries (if you'd call them that) were gone. Her nasty side came out, "Oh… so you're pushing me down in seniority?"

I sat there with my earbuds in my hand and thought about my response. Making enemies during my first month was not how I wanted to start my time on the west coast. But Shelley was not making that an easy decision. "Well, if you're junior to me, I guess I am pushing you down in seniority. That's how it usually works."

I put my earbuds back in thinking the conversation was over. It was not.

"Do you support the union?"

"What?"

She repeated herself. I kept my right earbud in trying politely to show that I was not in the mood to talk. She didn't care.

"I don't like the union. So, I guess I don't support them."

"Well, you really should. The union is here to help us."

Remember how I talked about first impressions? She officially had made a bad one. Union talk is like religion and politics talk. These discussions go both ways and both people involved must want to discuss it. Those are the three things I refuse to talk about at work. Religion. Politics. Unions. Want to discuss anal and alcohol? I am all ears. I love AA. But those other three are dangerous subjects, especially when you have different opinions.

I decided to end the conversation right there, "Yeah. I'm not a union guy. Nice talking to you." And I placed my earbuds back in my ear and ignored her while she stirred her coffee.

She eventually disappeared. But not for good.

A month later, I walked onto an airplane to commute home, and she was the lead flight attendant.

"Do I know you?" She asked as I pulled myself onto the airplane.

If I didn't want to get home quickly, I would have caught another flight. "Yeah. We met last month in the crew lounge." Then I pointed at my name bar.

"Oh right. The no-union guy. Where are you seated?"

"In the exit row. Nice seeing you again." Confession… that was a lie.

I put my earbuds in my ears and listened to Hall & Oats for the flight home. After we landed, I helped clean up the airplane for the flight back. Five of us ran through collecting trash and organizing the rows while Shelley made her way to the middle of the aircraft. She was relentless, and seemed to be targeting me, "Hey Joe, how long have you been here?"

That again. "I've been here for seven years."

"That's what I thought," she said, "I was telling the other flight attendant that you hadn't been here that long. Billy said you'd been here a long time, but you're not senior. For some reason, I thought you were here longer, but you haven't been." And just to make sure I heard her, she repeated it, "You haven't been here that long."

What the fuck crawled up this troll's ass and died? Did she hate me for some reason? Was it because I didn't like unions? Was it because I got more dick than her? That couldn't be the case; if she disliked gay male flight attendants, she'd need to transfer to someplace like Wichita, or Moscow.

Billy, the other flight attendant, piped in, "Don't involve me."

I stopped cleaning and pulled my gloves off. I walked up to Shelley, placed the gloves in her garbage bag, and said as nasty as possible, "I'm more senior than you, and that's all that matters." I stepped past her, grabbed my bags from the overhead bin, and walked off the airplane.

After those two run-ins, you can see why I was hesitant about working a trip with her. She apparently had a boner for seniority, and after our two other interactions, I was curious how the two-day trip would play out. And more importantly, whether she'd bring up seniority.

Shelley did not disappoint. While briefing in the crew lounge she asked, "How long have you been here?"

I became salty, "You do realize we've had this conversation twice, right? If you can't remember, I'm not telling you again."

"We have? Oh wait, we have." The lights in the crew lounge flickered, I expect her brain started working, "That's right. How could I forget?"

"I have no clue."

We boarded the airplane and found a fellow flight attendant, Theresa, in the front galley. Her bags were already in the overhead bin, and she was — get this shit — completing Shelley's security checks. Theresa was all smiles, so I expected she was over her Santa hat fiasco. I sure the hell wasn't, but I left it alone. She wasn't working the flight with us. Technically, she shouldn't have been allowed onboard because the working crew (me, Shelley, etc.) were not on the airplane. And that's a fucking no-no. I'm sure if reported; a gate agent might lose their job over something like that.

As I walked to the back of the airplane and stepped into the galley, Theresa picked up the interphone and made an announcement, "Joe. I already did your checks back there, so you're all good."

Irritated and apparently not over the Santa hat incident, I responded back, "Thanks, but I'll do my checks."

As I put my bags away, I looked up to see Theresa bulldozing around Shelley and getting in her way in the front galley. She opened up the lavatory door, stuck her head in the flight deck, and was grabbing things out of the bin. When passengers started boarding, Theresa was up and down into the overhead bin like an unseasoned passenger. I was glad to be working in the back galley, or I'd have recommended that she sit her ass down.

After boarding was complete, Theresa planted herself in her seat, and I hoped she'd stay there for the entire flight. I'm usually not that nasty towards flight attendants, but we were flying to Miami, and dealing with her up and down like a yo-yo for six hours was not in my flight attendant manual.

Neither was dealing with Shelley's crazy ass. Working with Shelley and having Theresa on the flight was excessive, even for me.

Then Shelley walked to the back galley and, without skipping a beat, asked, "Joe, how long have you been here?"

Just for the record, this was the fourth time she'd asked me that question. I seriously started questioning if she was suffering a brain hemorrhage. And if so, that was a slow fucking bleed that had been going on for months.

"This is the fourth time you've asked me that. I have been here, at this airline, for seven years." I walked towards the aisle trying to distance myself. She got the hint. She barely made it past row 12 for the entire flight, which was perfectly fine with me.

You know who did make it past row 12? You guessed it, Theresa. As we prepared the galley for landing, Theresa walked to the back of the airplane and started shopping. I thought nothing of her being in the galley until I was at row 19, in the overhead bin, when I heard full Diet Coke cans slamming against each other. I turned and walked back into the galley, and there was Theresa, with three trash bags inside one another, loading up on Diet Cokes, orange juices, a few cartons of milk, some tea, and who fucking knows what else.

"You sure you grabbed everything you need?" I asked sarcastically as she put the last few cans of iced tea in the bag.

"Oh yes, I've got everything I need. I'm gonna be in Miami on special assignment, and I need to stock up my hotel room for the weekend." With that, she twisted the bag around until it was nice and tight, flung it over her shoulder, and walked up the aisle towards her seat.

That wasn't a Santa hat she was so upset about, it was a Grinch hat.

"Can you believe this shit?" I asked the mid-cabin flight attendant who sat in her jumpseat reading a magazine. She didn't respond because her jaw was on the floor. She shook her head in amazement, and then we both laughed out loud.

It's normal for us to take water off the airplane when we have layovers. Airlines have guidelines of what we can and can not take off the aircraft. At my airline, we are allowed to take a select number of complimentary drinks with us to the hotel. Because technically, we are still working, and management doesn't want to deal with dehydrated flight attendants. What we are not allowed to take are items that the airline sells, specifically alcohol. That's termination if they catch you doing that. And I won't say we've all done it, but… most have done it at one point in time.

Theresa hadn't taken any alcohol; she had just shopped like she was getting her WIC card stamped.

When we checked into the hotel, Shelley asked the mid-cabin flight attendant and me which van time we were taking in the morning. I lied and told her a later time than what I planned on taking. We were scheduled to fly from Miami to Houston and then to LAX, and I'd need time to recover from her. That night, I even hid in my hotel room. I slam-clicked fast. The idea of bumping into Shelley in the hallway gave me nightmares.

Seriously, I think I had a nightmare about her peeking out from under my bed asking, "How long have you been here? How long have you been here? HOW LONG HAVE YOU BEEN HERE?"

The next morning, I was up, showered, dressed, and pulling my luggage through the hotel like I was escaping an abusive husband. I stepped outside, left my bags in the back of the van for the driver, stepped onto the shuttle and was greeted by Shelley.

"You decided to take an early van, too? What a coincidence."

This chick was psychotic and psychic. Did this bitch read minds? If so, she'd have run screaming if she knew what I thought as I stepped onto the van and sat across from her.

There was no escaping this woman, "Let me get your number, Joe."

My first instinct was to lie. I could have said I lost my phone, but it was in my hand as she waited to take down my number. I caved in and gave her my number.

Take a lesson from me: never give out your number to a crazy flight attendant, which means any flight attendant, because we are all fucking insane.

On our flight to LAX, I managed to work through my frustrations with Shelley, and her asking me a thousand times — alright four, but it felt like a thousand — about my seniority. As long as she never texted or called me, I'd forgive everything up till this point.

As we started our approach into LAX, the engines roared, and the airplane began climbing again. It's frightening, even for seasoned flight attendants. It's called a go-around, and once the pilots figure things out, they make a friendly announcement alerting passengers, and the flight attendants, what happened.

Luckily for us — that's a smart-ass comment — we didn't have to wait for the captain because Shelley came over the intercom and projected her verbal diarrhea into my ears and everyone else on the airplane. It was almost incoherent.

Her announcement went something like this, "Ladies and gentlemen, nothing to worry about it. Probably just trying to avoid some birds. Maybe there was a deer on the runway? That happens. Yeah, that's probably it. Maybe the Santa Ana winds are giving us some trouble. We'll just fly around for a few and then land."

Appalled. Embarrassed. Furious. Those are a few words that described me as Shelley rambled on the interphone. If being secured in our jumpseat weren't mandatory, I'd have walked to the front of the airplane, and slapped her with an oxygen tank. Hell, if I'm getting terminated for striking a fellow flight attendant, I might as well take a few of her teeth with me.

I picked up the interphone and called her. Before she could respond, I unleashed, "What the hell are you doing? I can't believe you said that. That's so inappropriate."

The call went dead. Shelley either hung up on me — highly possible — or there was a problem with the interphone.

When we landed, I realized there was a chance to catch my flight home. Even with the go-around, we landed on time. But the passengers were deplaning slow enough to lose a snail race. As I paced back and forth in the back galley waiting to sprint and catch my flight home, the mid-flight attendant called me, "Joe, don't worry about your commute. You won't miss it."

I asked, "Why? What's up?"

"Shelley got tagged to work the San Jose turn tonight. So the flight isn't departing until she gets on the airplane.

I laughed out loud and realized I really couldn't get away from her.

After the passengers deplaned, I raced past her while she collected her bags and cheerfully said, "See you on the flight."

She asked, "You're going to San Jose? Why didn't they tag you to operate the flight?"

I smile, "Because I'm senior to you. And anyway, who would work the flight back?"

Something tells me she will never again ask how long I've been with the airline, and I am perfectly okay with that.

The Egomaniac Pilot

The departure gate at Tampa International Airport was a complete shit show. I instantly empathized with the gate agent as I walked up to the counter; she looked thoroughly flustered. Passengers surrounded the gate and were actively forcing their way to the front of the line. It was straight out of a horror movie. The only thing missing were the pitchforks, ski masks, and haunting music.

The departure board read:

Dallas
Flight 38
DELAYED

My eyes went straight to the word delayed typed out in bold lettering. That's not a shock. Have you heard the phrase, an open bottle of wine is an empty bottle of wine? Well, I have one for the airline industry: a scheduled departure flight is a delayed flight.

I placed my bags against the window and noticed there was no airplane parked at the gate. I walked up to the agent, "When is the airplane landing?"

She tapped away at her computer screen assisting the passenger standing over her, "What flight are you working?"

That was odd. I was in uniform, with my luggage, and standing at the Dallas gate. Maybe she thought I was going to Minneapolis. "I'm working the Dallas flight."

She snapped, "There's been a gate change. This gate isn't for Dallas."

Not that big of a deal. We have gate changes all the time. I waited a minute for the gate agent to inform me where the new gate was, but she said nothing.

"What's the new gate?

"I have no idea."

If I were that lackadaisical about my job, passengers would die; or worse, we'd run out of Dr. Pepper.

Finally, when she finished with the passenger standing in front of her, she picked up her walkie-talkie, "Gina, do you copy? What gate is Dallas going out of?"

Within seconds Gina responded, "Fourteen."

I thanked the frazzled gate agent, grabbed my luggage, and headed to the new gate. I have a great deal of respect for gate agents. Even when they get nasty and bitchy with me, I maintain my composure. Personally, I think being a gate agent is the worst job in the airline industry. I think it's harder than the person responsible for vacuuming out the piss and shit from the toilet tank. I could never do their job. Never! I'm talking about being a gate agent; I'd clean up shit before I'd stand at a gate smiling through countless delays and cancellations. The airline couldn't pay me enough to work at the gate or ticket counter and manage through the verbal lashings these passengers hand out. Sure, passengers are demanding on the airplane, that's a given, but in all honesty, passengers are much gentler on the plane than inside the airport. And let's face it, if passengers are assholes on the airplane, at the terminal they are the adult versions of *The Children of the Corn*.

When I walked up to gate 14, I was pleased to see the airplane parked and attached to the jet bridge. Captain Randall stood sipping his coffee and before I could smile, informed me that the aircraft we were looking at was not our airplane. Our plane hadn't landed yet; the airplane at the gate was departing to Detroit. We had to wait for that aircraft to leave, ours to arrive, and pull up to the gate before we could start our day.

I set my luggage against the wall behind the podium to stay away from the onslaught of irate passengers' eyes shooting at us like poisonous darts. Passengers are vultures when there is a delay. True, they are vultures all the time, but when there's a delay, they get hungry for information. And when they reach the point of starvation, they feed off flight attendants, pilots, gate agents, and anyone else they can sink their beak into. Once, in Atlanta, I witnessed a woman ask the restroom attendant why her flight hadn't departed. The restroom attendant? She barely knows why the soap dispenser is empty. That's desperation. When you are frantic enough to ask the lady cleaning the toilets about your flight you've hit what I like to call airline passenger rock bottom.

That's why I set up camp behind the gate and refuse to make eye contact. I avoid the sea of people congregating around for fear that one of them will catch my attention, and conclude it's perfectly fine to barrage me with their passenger questions that I don't care to answer. When eye contact is established, it's all over. The passenger will beeline directly to you — even if you are chewing on a turkey sandwich — and violate your lunch, "Why is the airplane late?"

"I don't know."

"When are we leaving?"

"I couldn't tell you."

"Do I have time to get coffee?"

"Fuck off! I'm eating a turkey sandwich."

After waiting at gate 14 for 30 minutes, the confused gate agent was back and announced another gate change. Without smiling, she made a standoffish PA, "Ladies and gentlemen, this is a gate change announcement. Flight 38 to Dallas will now be departing from gate 28. Thank you."

People pushed past each other like it was Black Friday at Walmart. Why the rush? Where do people think they are going without the flight attendants and pilots? Nowhere. The five of us — three flight attendants and two pilots — maintained a decent ten feet of distance behind the mad dash to the new gate.

When we stepped onto the airplane, we quickly realized it was one of the oldest airplanes in our fleet. The hunk of metal was older than my nursing and flight attendant careers combined. The worst part was there was no wifi or live entertainment options for the passengers. It seemed we not only swapped gates twice, but we also swapped airplanes twice, and the only aircraft left in Tampa was a turd with two engines.

"Brent, this airplane is a piece of shit." one of the flight attendants said to the first officer as we walked on.

He laughed, "As long as it's a piece of shit that gets us to our destination."

I assume that's important for passengers, getting to their destination in one piece and not ending up at the

bottom of the Gulf of Mexico. You'd think that was important, but it's not. Or at least it doesn't seem to be paramount when talking with airline passengers on the airplane. Do you know what's more crucial than surviving the flight? Having a television to watch and wifi to post lavatory selfies on Instagram. I hate to admit it, but from the way passengers act on the airplane when their television or the wifi is not working leads me to believe what I say is gospel. I often wonder if the traveling public would rather the airline cancel the flight than depart with inoperative televisions or wifi. It's broken wifi and a seven-inch television, not a wing. There's not a day that doesn't go by where I think about picking up the intercom and screaming at 100 passengers, "The televisions stopped working. Settle down! Why are you crying like we lost both engines on our way to Hawaii?"

I need my job, so I just say that to myself. It helps.

After we boarded the flight, we learned one of the overhead bins wouldn't close. It was the overhead bin over row 20. Paula, the mid-cabin flight attendant, made several attempts to close the overhead bin, but each time it popped right back open.

Close. Pop open. Close. Pop open. Close. Pop open. She looked at me and shrugged her shoulders. I swayed back and forth from the back galley as my patience ran thinner and thinner. We were already 45 minutes delayed, which was ruining my chances of commuting home on the early flight.

If it's not one thing, it's another.

Management continually reminds us of the importance of flights departing on time. Unfortunately, they rarely leave on time. I can be scheduled six days in a row, and work 20 flights, and not one of them depart on time. That's not an exaggeration — that's reality. And the blame lands on the flight attendants, pilots, and gate agents. I guess that makes sense; it's easier for management to blame the worker bees than having the CEO standing out on the tarmac screaming at Mother Nature for so many Florida thunderstorms.

In all honesty, after making money and paying the shareholders, on-time performance is indispensable to the airlines. If an airplane crashed in the Atlantic Ocean, they'd sit around their conference table talking about whether it departed on time or took a delay. In initial flight attendant training, they shoved that information down our throats.

Paula gave up on the overhead bin and walked to the back, "It won't close. The spring isn't working."

Today was starting to suck more than a Republican politician in a restroom stall.

I picked up the interphone and called the flight deck, "Hey guys. This is Joe. We have a bin that won't close."

Randall sounded annoyed. "Why are you just telling us now? We're about to close the door."

I took a deep breath, "I'm telling you now because we just tried closing it and the spring isn't working."

There was a pause, "Brent is coming to the back to check it out."

Brent meandered down the aisle and hovered at row 20. The passengers observed him with intensity, while I watched with annoyance.

Close. Pop open. Close. Pop open. Close. Pop open. Paula walked up to him, and I watched as they stood there with thumbs up their asses. Randall must not have had much faith in Brent — if that's the case, I hope Randall was flying that day — because, at that moment, maintenance stormed down the aisle towards Tweedle Paula and Tweedle Brent.

Maintenance was about as helpful as a blind crossing guard. Close. Pop open. Close. Pop open. Close. Pop open. All three of them stood there with their hands on their hips as if to say; this may be the most challenging problem we ever solve.

I was fucking done.

I walked up the aisle, pushed myself past the three of them, moved the two pieces of luggage to another bin, and announced, "Just tape it up so we can get out of here."

Do you know how long it takes to slap two pieces of goddamn duct tape on an overhead bin to label it inoperative? The answer is too long. Way too fucking long. It took 15 minutes to duct tape the overhead bin and another 20 minutes for maintenance to write it up in the logbook. In case you are unaware, anything broken on the airplane must get logged in a book. And for reasons I don't fully understand, this process takes forever. I know that 35 minutes is not forever, but when you are trying to fly across the country to catch your commute home, 35 minutes is an eternity. Apparently, maintenance men have a knack for taking their sweet ass time writing a sentence. That's why you will never find a book titled, Airline Maintenance Max Tells All because it would take him 25 years to write out the dedication.

08/4/14. Placed two pieces of duct tape on the overhead bin because it will not stay closed. Max.

It took me 15 seconds to write that sentence.

Things went south quickly after we departed. Before boarding began, the gate agent made several announcements regarding the televisions and wifi, specifically that they were inoperative on the flight. But do airline passengers listen to announcements?

Nope. Nobody listens to shit unless we're announcing free drinks. Each passenger that I approached, and ones that I didn't, asked about the televisions. It wasn't random passengers in separated rows who asked, it was people seated next to each other:

Me, "Hi. May I get you something to drink?"

18A, "Do you know why my television screen is out?"

Me, "The televisions aren't working on this flight. I'm sorry."

18A (growling), "It would have been nice if they'd have told us that before we got on the airplane."

Me, "They did. There was an announcement at the gate. May I get you something to drink?"

Then when I turned my head two inches and addressed 18B, "Hi. Would you care for something to drink?"

18B, "Do you know why my tv screen is out?"

"The same reason that 18A's screen is out. The televisions are not working."

"It would have been nice if they told us that before..."

You get where this is going. That happened 50 times while I took drink orders. It was so time-consuming that I was practically handing out Sprites while landing in Dallas.

Then some fat bearded dude walked to the back, looked at me, and said, "Can I hit that?"

Was he talking about me, or the lavatory? God, I hoped it was the lavatory. I nodded my head and pointed to the toilet. He erupted in a creepy rapist laugh, "I love you, Joe."

The guy wasn't ugly, but he smelled like pickles and looked like he had spent his summer vacationing behind an airport dumpster.

Later on during the flight, he asked for a cranberry juice. When I delivered it to his seat, I also brought him a bottle of water and encouraged him to stay hydrated.

As I walked away, out of the corner of my eye, I caught him toss a $5.00 bill on the tray table. What did he think $5.00 bought him? Flight Attendant Joe riding his smelly pickle for the next two hours? I paused for a moment, took a deep breath, and stepped back one row until I was standing beside his aisle seat. I picked up the $5.00, looked at it, and handed it back to him.

"We aren't allowed to accept tips, but thank—"

Before I finished my sentence, I saw two mini bottles sticking out of his seat back pocket. Then, as if he owned the airplane and answered to no one, he pulled another bottle out from his front shirt pocket, cracked it open, and poured the entire contents into his cup of ice.

His level of arrogance struck me square in the jaw. "Sir, you know it's a federal offense to serve yourself alcohol on the airplane?"

He looked up, shot me a flirty grin, and answered, "Yes, Joe. I know all about the FAA."

Was this guy for real? "That's great. I'm glad you know all about the FAA. But if you bring your alcohol on the airplane, you have to tell me, and I have to serve it to you."

Let me clarify; it's not like that at all airlines. Some airlines don't allow you to bring any liquor on the airplane. It doesn't matter who serves it to you. But my airline is more lenient. We allow passengers to carry on alcohol, but as per the FAA, we must serve it to the passenger. What

225

does that mean? That means, at my airline, if you bring minis from home with you, you merely tell the flight attendant, hand over the minis, and the flight attendant will serve you.

I know you probably have a headache and want me to pay for your ibuprofen, but there is a reason for all this nonsense.

Safety! Safety is our top priority. Shocked? You thought our top priority was delivering you a cup of coffee on a 30-minute flight. Am I right? Serving you that cup of Joe is part of our job, but it's not our number one priority. Safety is our numero uno responsibility. Knowing exactly how much alcohol each passenger ingests is crucial for a safe flight. That's why we must serve ALL adult beverages on the airplane. You may be the best bartender in Ybor City, but on the airplane, we are the bartender. If left in the dark about your alcohol consumption, we'll be scratching our heads in the back galley wondering why you're slurring your words and projectile vomiting all over the lady in 21C. Or why you've passed out. Or pissed on the little boy sitting next to you. Or choked on your vomit and died in your seat.

He placed the empty mini on the tray table, "Well, this is all of it. I don't have anymore."

I spent enough time talking to him to realize he was at his limit, "Good. Do you think you've had enough?"

"Maybe."

I clasped my hands together, "The answer is, yes. You've had enough to drink. Are you sure you don't have any more minis?

"No, Joe. I don't." He poured the cranberry juice into the Tito's vodka.

"Okay. Please don't drink anymore. We will be landing soon."

He smiled, "I love you, Joe."

He reached out to shake my hand. When I shook it, it was wet. Gross.

We were flying the same airplane to California. During our initial descent into Dallas, a passenger walked to the back galley to use the lavatory. He stopped before opening the door, "Are the televisions going to be fixed in Dallas?"

He was addressing me, but Paula jumped in. "You never know. They might."

I immediately corrected her, "No. They won't fix the TVs today. We're only in Dallas long enough to deplane, refuel, reboard new passengers, and leave. That's about all the time we'll have."

Being the bearer of that bad news — when there was a high probability I'd miss my commute — made me happy. The man stepped into the lavatory and closed the door. Paula looked over at me, "They might fix the TVs. I've seen it done before."

She irritated me, "You've seen it done before? You've seen them fix an entire airplane in-flight entertainment system during a 40 minute turn?"

"I think I have." Her story changed rapidly. I wasn't convinced.

"Where? Where did that happen?"

She thought, "I think it was JFK."

"Well yeah, they probably can fix it in one of our hubs, but not in Dallas, Texas."

She giggled, "Oh yeah, that makes sense."

Working with new hires takes years off your life.

Then she continued, "I just hate that the passengers are upset there are no TVs. They pay for TVs."

"They pay to get to Dallas or LA. The TVs are just a bonus. I don't think anyone woke up today and said, 'I think I wanna watch the game on an airplane.'"

"Why are you so snippy?" A new flight attendant and already calling out my attitude. I realized she'd go far as a flight attendant once she got some seniority behind her.

"I have a commute to catch when we get to LA. I had plenty of time, but all these delays have made it close."

"I'm sure you'll be fine," she said. Then she handed a bottle of water to the guy who walked out of the lavatory.

She was right. I'd be fine. If I missed my original plan, there was a later flight I'd be able to catch. Honestly, I didn't mind waiting in the airport, there was a wine bar located in our terminal, but if I could make the earlier flight to San Jose, I'd jump on it faster than a fat white cop on a black elementary school kid.

After a quick turn in Dallas, we dropped off a few Texas Republicans and replaced them with a few more Texas Republicans. While we boarded, a female passenger walked to the back galley and immediately pissed me off. Her expression frustrated me before she had the opportunity to open her mouth and make the situation worse.

"Are you kidding me?" She asked putting her hands on her hips and tilting her head, "No TVs for the entire flight? That's ridiculous."

She pronounced her words slowly, but not in the friendly Texas way with which I've become familiar. There was no, "Howdy." No, "How y'all doing?" No, "Out of my way queer, this restroom is for straights only."

Nothing.

That disappointed me, but I smiled, "Nobody is kidding. Been there and done that today. We flew from Florida with no television and everybody survived."

Mrs. Texas gave me a look like she had already written a complaint letter and received approval from the airline to rip the wings off my chest. As she glared my way, I concluded that when — not if — but when I received the call to report to my supervisor's office for this interaction, I'd own it with pride. In all my years as a flight attendant, I have never received a complaint letter. How is that possible? I have no clue. It's more of a mystery than the disappearance of Malaysia Airlines flight 370. Out of all the interactions that I've encountered on the airplane, and we are talking well over 200,000 (trust me, I did the math) and counting, none have resulted in a complaint letter. Not one single passenger has written in a letter to complain about my conduct. That seems odd to me, not because I think I'm a raging asshole who lashes out at every passenger I meet — I only lash out at abusive passengers — but because I have seen complaint letters written against flight attendants for something as innocent as forgetting to bring a passenger a bottle of water. I figured that if an airline passenger took time out of their hectic schedule to complain about that, there's no doubt in my mind that this Texan bitch was ready to accuse me of sins against humanity for telling her that other passengers survived their flight without watching *Big Brother 16*. As I said, I'd deserve the letter, and I'd proudly parade it around like a flag at the San Francisco Pride Parade.

Halfway through the flight to Los Angeles, the pilots needed a break, so I went up to relieve them with Rebecca.

Rebecca, the lead flight attendant, wanted to stay out and guard the flight deck, so I went inside and started chatting with Randall.

He was extremely friendly, "How's it going back there?"

"It's good," I pulled out my phone, "Do you mind if I take a few pictures out the window?" It's rare that I go up into the flight deck and not take at least one picture. He nodded, and I started snapping pictures of the ground below. I continued the conversation, "These delays have messed up my flight home. I'm probably going to miss my commute."

Without any pause, he responded, "Just run off the airplane once we park at the gate."

I stopped taking pictures and slowly put the phone back in my pocket. I gazed at Randall for a brief moment to collect my thoughts. To be honest, it upsets me that the pilots at my airline have no clue about our work rules. I don't expect them to memorize the flight attendant pay scale, or how many hours we have to work in a month, but they should know if we are allowed to leave the airplane while passengers are still in their seats. All I'm saying is that if pilots want to walk around with their chests puffed out talking about being in command, then they should know the ins and outs of when and where their flight attendants should be during a flight. All the flight attendants working must remain on the airplane until every last passenger has deplaned. If we walk off the airplane before that occurs, management will terminate us. No second chances. No saying, "I'm sorry." No saying, "Please give me another chance. I need this job." It's like a female in Saudi Arabia trying to convince her father that she needs to keep her clitoris. Nope! We're cut from the schedule quicker than that flap of skin. That's why flight attendants moan and groan — not because of the clitoris thing — but when passengers crawl off the airplane like they have no place to go.

I finally answered, "I can't do that. I'll get fired."

"Well, I won't report you."

Eerily, it felt like having a conversation with a creepy uncle who asks you to touch his squishy penis at the family reunion, and when you hesitate he says, "I won't tell."

Or something like that.

"Thanks, but I'm not doing that." I wanted to tell him to fly the airplane as fast as possible and let me deal with catching my flight home.

When we landed, I waited until the last passenger strolled off the airplane before I started pulling down my luggage from the overhead bin. I focused on breathing, staying calm, and being mindful of my situation. I am the worst at commuting. I believe every commute takes a few minutes off my life. At the rate I'm going, I hope I live to finish this book.

Rebecca was not helping my peaceful state. She picked up the interphone and shouted throughout the airplane, "Joe, hurry up. Come on! You can do it. Hurry! Hurry! Hurry!

I hadn't rushed like that since trying to have sex on the side of the road in a Toyota Camry. These two were way too invested in my commute home. What I needed was for them to calm down before they gave me a heart attack. You know it's terrible when the stress of your coworkers rooting for you is more overwhelming than missing your flight.

I bolted down the aisle with my luggage and thanked her as I ran off the airplane towards the terminal. Lucky for me, my flight was at gate 11, which was the next gate over. As I sprinted to the gate out of breath, Randall had his arms folded on the counter shaking his head at me as if I was caught doing something terrible.

Before I had a chance to express myself he spoke, "You missed the flight. I'm sorry. I tried to hold it for you, but they wouldn't do it."

Catching my breath, I placed my luggage next to the counter, "Thank you. It's cool. I don't expect the pilots to hold the flight for a non-paying passenger. But thanks anyway."

Randall wouldn't let up, "How are these people not going to hold the flight for you?" When he began raising his voice at the gate agent, I politely directed him away from the gate. He rattled on and was unable to control himself. Why was he upset? It was my commute, not his. When we were a few feet away from the gate agent, I thanked him — for what seemed like the tenth time — and walked away towards the gate where the next flight to San Jose was departing. Once I separated myself from Randall and checked in for the next flight, I disappeared into the restroom to change out of my uniform so I could enjoy a juicy hamburger and a few glasses of red wine at the restaurant while waiting for the next flight.

That was my saving grace. A few months prior, I had missed a commuting flight and was beside myself. If I had been a toddler, I'd have spent five minutes throwing my luggage around, grabbing things off the counter and tossing them at the gate agent, and ending the tantrum on the ground pounding my fists until they bled. When the emotional storm passed, it became clear that I only had to wait three hours for the next flight. There was no need to burn down the airport. All I needed was a glass of wine. I changed, found a restaurant that not only served wine, but served an extremely mouth-watering burger, and the three hours went by in a flash.

When I came out of the restroom in my civilian clothes, Randall's voice was audible from every direction. He continued to preach about the incident to any flight attendant or pilot who walked by him in their uniform and spoke loud enough for the gate agents to hear him. This entire fiasco made me extremely uncomfortable. As I advanced towards him and his audience, it became clear that Randall was a few playing cards short of a full deck.

I quietly strolled up to him. He stood reiterating the tale to two flight attendants I had worked with in the past. They looked at me with confusion and fear; I looked at them with frustration and guilt. How did I instantly become this guy's handler?

Randall's neck was fire engine red, and his eyes bulged from their sockets like that scene in *Total Recall* when Arnold Schwarzenegger gets tossed out into the Mars landscape with no oxygen. If that wasn't crazy enough, he reminded me of someone who was about to shoot up the airport because a flight canceled. Was Randall a Federal Flight Deck Officer? Did he carry a gun? I checked my memory and was relieved that he informed us in Tampa that he was not authorized to carry a firearm. I guess those psychiatric evaluations do make a difference.

"How could that captain not listen to me? And what about the gate agents? We board early for them when they ask? We do everything for these gate agents, and they can't hold the flight for my flight attendant?"

I jumped it. "Nobody can hold a flight for a standby flight attendant."

He ignored me and continued addressing the two female flight attendants, "When I flew for my previous airline, we'd drop the airstairs for standby passengers on the runway."

That triggered me. Apparently, someone forgot to take their medication that morning, and that someone was not me. Randall wasn't right in the head, and as I continued listening to his ranting, I realized significant plot holes were missing from his story.

I felt sorry for the two flight attendants trapped in his spider web of crazy, but I excused myself from their huddle and walked over to the gate to find out exactly what occurred before I arrived.

I'm glad I did.

The three gate agents behind the counter looked at me with contempt as I forced a smile on my face, "Hey, I don't know what's going on, but I have nothing to do with this nonsense."

One of the male gate agents spoke up, "He's gone too far. We can hear everything he's saying. He was extremely disrespectful to the crew, to us, and he continues with this behavior."

As the gate agent spoke, I could still hear Mount Randall erupting about 10 feet away.

"What did he do?" I asked.

"He went down the jet bridge stairs, ran across the tarmac to the other airplane, went up the stairs and blocked the gate agent from closing the door stating he had a flight attendant who was trying to catch the flight."

I could barely breathe. I may have shit a little in my underwear.

He continued, "He pushed past the gate agent and went inside the flight deck and told the captain to hold the airplane for you because you were running to catch the flight."

Nope. I think I shit myself after hearing that. Words escaped me. I was numb from the throat up.

Then the female gate agent interrupted, "We are filing a report against him, and we'll be including you in the report."

I found a few words, "What? Why am I included?"

"You are the reason this happened. We have to report this to the chief pilot at JFK. It's a violation to run across the tarmac attempting to stop an airplane from departing."

"Sure, I get that, but you don't have to include my name."

Who tries stopping an airplane from departing? I'd have to figure out how to never fly with this nutcase again, but first, I had to process what was going on at the gate. I know how shit goes down in the airline industry. Pilots are rarely held accountable for their actions. I've witnessed pilots disrespect passengers, flight attendants, and gate agents with zero reprimands for their actions. Plain and simple, the airline industry is the reason pilots have a God complex. On the flip side of that, guess who is held accountable for everything? You guessed it, flight attendants. Flight delayed? Blame the flight attendant. A broken television. That's the flight attendant's fault. Ran out of Diet Coke on a Buffalo flight? Damn fight attendants, they should count and make sure we have enough Diet Coke provisioned.

My imagination went wild standing at the gate thinking of how this would all end up on my shoulders. I have big shoulders, but even I can't hold up a crazy airline captain.

"You have nothing to worry about," the male gate agent said, "This is all on him. You're just a witness."

True statement. My ass was still on the airplane while Randall went postal and violated numerous safety rules. That truth didn't help the matter; I freaked about being associated with this stupidity. I'm a blogger. It's important I stay under the radar and not bring attention to myself, which if you know me personally, you know that statement is about as authentic as lips on a real housewife.

The gate agent was correct. To this day, I've never heard anything further regarding the incident.

I left the gate conflicted. Slightly embarrassed, but also somewhat honored that a pilot would get crazy for me. A little Stockholm syndrome vibe. What made him take ownership of the situation? The entire experience boggled my mind. It's rare that I even have a pilot tell me to take my jumpseat during turbulence, and this captain ran across the tarmac and risked being scolded by management for me. Was he looking to be a hero? Did he think he was Superman? Fuck, did he think I was Lois Lane?

Maybe he just wanted some ass.

I never found out. When I finally walked away from the gate, Randall was gone. The show was over. I sauntered over to the restaurant, found a seat facing the terminal, and watched passengers meander around the airport while enjoying two glasses of red wine.

It took me a few hours, and those two glasses of red wine, to put everything into perspective. Clarity about Randall came clear once I was seated on the flight and halfway to San Jose. His rage had nothing to do with me and my commute. He didn't give two shits about, Joe, and the fact that I missed my flight and spent an additional three hours in the airport. A relaxing three hours spent sipping wine and reading a book. Randall was angry because when he walked on the other airplane and asked the captain to hold the flight to San Jose, the captain did not do what he requested. The gate agents didn't collapse at his feet and bow to his demands. This became crystal clear when I remembered that he ignored me when I reminded him that the airline would not hold a flight for a standby flight attendant. He knew that all along. Everyone in the airline industry knows that you can't demand the gate agents, pilots, or flight attendants to delay a flight for standby passengers.

His massive ego drove Randall. An ego that took over, lashing out at anyone within earshot of his conversation. Ego doesn't care about relationships or your job. It certainly doesn't care about the aftermath it leaves behind as you awaken from the haze it created inside your brain. In Ryan Holiday's book *Ego is the Enemy* he writes, "The bigger the ego, the harder the fall." As my flight started descending towards San Jose International Airport, I couldn't help but laugh at the idea of Randall, not merely falling hard from that event, but being kicked out of the airplane and free falling to the ground from 38,000 feet. That's most likely how it felt for him when his ego took a kick to the balls at gate 11. To this day, it still amazes me how involved he was in my business. All he had to do was walk out of the airport, catch the van to the hotel, and call it a night. Instead, he sent Brent to the hotel and took it upon himself to save my night, and when it didn't work, he had a meltdown in the airport.

I still think he wanted my ass.

The Homophobe Who Murdered His Ostrich

Lesson #1: When the gate agent boards the airplane and informs you that one of your passengers recently put down their pet ostrich, take my word for it that the passenger will be over-the-top difficult.

Lesson #2: Refrain from asking how the ostrich was put down.

Don't say I didn't warn you when you ask and find out the passenger killed his ostrich by putting a hose down its throat to drown it. Whether this is the humane way to euthanize an ostrich, I have no clue, but I believe that drowning is a terrible way to die. I hear it's excruciating.

Just ask anyone who's endured an afternoon of water-boarding at Guantanamo Bay.

"He killed his ostrich?" I asked looking at the lead flight attendant, Coco, "That's a first for me."

"That's not all," the gate agent said standing in the galley next to the lavatory, "Ricky's in a wheelchair, he's had some drinks, and he'd like to board last because he's traveling with his cousin, Bobby, who has explosive diarrhea."

"Are you lying? That's crazy. Wheelchairs board first."
I challenged her waiting for her to scream — GOTCHA!

She ensured us she was not lying.

I will go on record and state that this was not a fabricated conversation. It may seem like it was, and that I am making this story up as I go, but I promise you that I am not.

Coco sipped on his iced coffee, "I was hoping for a pleasant flight."

I peered down the jet bridge and then stepped back into the front galley, "If one of these country bumpkins has Ebola, I'm gonna be pissed."

Flight attendants and pilots have the right to refuse any passenger to board who is actively sick; Coco and I needed to see these two passengers with our own eyes.

Coco put down his iced coffee, "Come on, let's run up to the gate and scope these guys out."

"Sounds like an adventure. Let me grab my crew badge."

We walked up to the gate and instantly spotted the two passengers seated across from the counter. Ricky in his wheelchair and his cousin seated next to him. I was more worried about, Bobby, the guy with explosive diarrhea than, Ricky, the guy who drowned his ostrich. Let me remind you; we're not just talking regular diarrhea. We are talking explosive diarrhea. I hate being one of those nitpicky flight attendants, but I never allow anything that explodes on the airplane.

We walked right up to Bobby, "Hi," I said, "We're two of the flight attendants on today's flight to Los Angeles. Are you feeling up to flying today?"

Ricky jumped in, "Oh my cousin is fine. Nothing to worry about."

We ignored him. Coco directed his statement to Bobby, "We just want to make sure you are safe to fly."

Bobby answered in a soft voice, "Oh yeah, I'm feeling much better."

Coco and I watched the two cowboys for a few seconds and made the executive decision to allow Bobby to travel. Secretly, I wondered if he wore adult diapers and knew how to change them himself. I'm known for going above and beyond, but I draw the line at changing a shitty cowboy's diaper.

Boarding commenced, and as requested, Ricky and Bobby were allowed to board last. We watched Ricky limp from his wheelchair to the airplane door with an unsteady gait. Ricky clumsily stepped from the jet bridge into the galley, grabbing anything secured to the airplane. I approached him ready to assist, and while holding onto the overhead bin with his right hand, he reached over and grabbed for my shoulder with the left. His fingernails looked like talons, which caught me off guard. As he moved, I got a glimpse of Edward Scissorhands coming towards me, and my body reacted. I tried playing it cool, but my instincts kicked in causing me to flinch, which practically sent me headfirst into the tits of the lady sitting in 1D. I'm not ashamed to admit yellow fingernails that look like they belonged to Count Dracula freak me the fuck out. And besides the frightful bird claw, how did I not know if that was the same hand he used to place the hose down his beloved ostrich's neck?

Things seemed to be going well once the flight closed up and we departed for Los Angeles. Thankfully, there were no ostriches on board for Ricky to slaughter. No ostrich killing sprees on my plane, that's for sure. He remained seated in 5C and spent the first part of the flight emptying out the entire contents of his carry on bag while cousin Bobby re-positioned his cowboy hat every few minutes. At that point during the trip, my focus was solely on Bobby. This redneck was a ticking shit bomb on a three a half hour flight.

Anything was possible.

During beverage service, Coco sauntered to the back galley to let us know that Ricky ordered a beer.

"What's the big deal? He didn't seem drunk to me." I responded while turning around to focus on Coco.

Coco continued, "Ricky told me he has a neurological disorder and that he usually takes medications, but that he's off them right now."

"No shit he has a neurological disorder… he drowned an ostrich."

Coco laughed, "Right? That's too much." He leaned against the back jump seat, "I just don't know what to do with this guy. And now he's saying his head hurts and he wants ice for it."

At that moment, a light bulb went off above all three of our heads simultaneously.

"I don't think we should be serving this guy any alcohol. The gate agent said he had drinks. He's complaining about his head hurting and has brain problems. I think we should stay away from the alcohol."

Regal chimed in, "I agree with Joe. Offer him water."

Coco grabbed a bottle of water off the galley counter, 'That's what I'm going to do. Just wanted to run it by you guys in case he asks one of you for alcohol."

I smiled and turned back around to the galley counter, "He ain't getting shit from me."

Ten minutes later, Coco stormed to the back galley in distress.

Before I go any further, let me set the record straight, Coco is an incredible flight attendant. He can handle any situation that presents itself in that metal tube. I bet you that if the airplane were plummeting towards the ocean in a blaze of glory, Coco would personally deliver the lady in 2A her Coke Zero before impact. That's the type of flight attendant he is, while everyone else is screaming and trying to grab onto the oxygen masks — he's finishing service with a smile.

I was seated in my jumpseat having a snack when Coco stepped in the galley. He was livid as he spun around and rested himself against the galley counter, "This guy is working my last nerve. I told him very politely that I wouldn't serve him any alcohol due to the information he gave me…"

He grabbed a bottle of water, took a swig, and caught his breath. I had never seen him this mad at a passenger. Immediately caught up in his drama, I continued stuffing grapes into my mouth like breath mints.

"But as I tried handing him a bottle of water he brushed me off and told me to leave him alone."

"And that upsets you?" I asked putting my grapes down, "You should be happy he doesn't want to talk to you."

"Joe, that's not the point. He shouldn't be rude like that."

I stood up, "Yes. I get it but don't let that asshole bother you. Fuck it." I looked over at Regal, "Right?"

She stood up and placed her hand on his shoulder, "Don't let him bother you. He's an asshole."

"Let me go through and pick up trash. I wanna see if that fucker will say something to me." Stepping into the front galley, I grabbed a garbage bag and started slowly down the aisle picking up cans and cups along the way. When I approached row five, I made eye contact with cousin Bobby and smiled. Without hesitation, he turned his head to look out the window. His reaction didn't phase me. I believe I've read somewhere in the *Texan Citizen's Handbook*, under the men's section, deep inside the chapter — How To Survive Contact With A Gay — that it says explicitly never to make eye contact with a gay guy for fear of being immediately converted into a cock-craving homosexual. Perhaps he feared even the slightest eye contact with me would leave him longing for a dick in his mouth.

Not my dick, but someone's dick. He's from Texas, so probably cousin Ricky's. I have no clue; I was just happy he hadn't shit himself. Handling cranky old Ricky seemed simple enough, but managing cranky old Ricky while his cousin sat three feet from him with a pile of barbecue pork in his underwear, that sounded like an emergency diversion into the Grand Canyon.

Ricky looked up from fingering around the junk he had dumped onto the seat separating him and Bobby. From the looks of it, he was going to Los Angeles to audition for a spot on the television show, *Let's Make A Deal*. If Wayne Brady asked a contestant for a pack of Marlboro Reds, a few used cotton balls, or a Walmart Gift Card, Ricky would have won what was behind curtain number three.

I made a hard stop at the row and politely asked, "Do you have any trash you need me to take?" My instinct was to scoop up everything into the trash bag, including Ricky, but I paused waiting for him to answer.

When he did, he completely ignored my question. Now that I think about it, he probably never heard me in the first place. He garbled, "Hey, who's the stewardess on the flight?"

I smiled, "We don't have a stewardess on this flight. We're all flight attendants. May I help you?"

He pointed to the front of the airplane, "The guy in the front won't serve me a beer. I want a beer."

I looked over towards Bobby, who was quite happy avoiding any interaction on the airplane. As cordial as I've ever been, I answered, "That is correct, Ricky. All three of us agreed that because of your medical history and the fact that you are slurring your words, we would not be serving you alcohol on this flight. May I bring you something else?"

Always the gentlemen flight attendant, I felt that offering him another option, like Coco had, was the professional and responsible way to handle the situation. Ricky wanted no part of my genteel behavior. He countered with, "I want to speak to the captain about this."

I held back my laughter. Alright, I let out a prominent chuckle. The older I get, the harder it is holding back my true feelings when it comes to the stupidity of these airline passengers. I guess that's why the airlines pay their flight attendants significantly more money the longer we stay, because the longer we spend in a metal tube with these assholes, the harder we work at not telling them to fuck off.

Without breaking character, because most flight attendants (including myself) are fake when dealing with passenger drama, I replied, "The captain is flying the airplane. He won't get involved with our decision not to serve you alcohol."

At that second, if I had been outside the airplane — say on the wing enjoying a latte — I'd have heard the seven trumpets sound and witness the four horsemen galloping alongside the aircraft. My remark to Ricky opened the seventh seal of the Rickocalypse.

In that instant, the devil came outta Mr. Ricky, "Go away. I don't want to talk to you two guys. If either one of you guys talks to me again, I will report you for sexual harassment."

That's all I needed to hear. I spun around on my heels and headed straight to the front galley to call the pilots and request security to meet the airplane when we landed.

I was angry. No, I was beyond angry, I'd call it enraged. With my ears red, chest burning, and neck sweating I barely held onto the interphone waiting for the pilots to answer the call. My body shook as I fought the urge to lift Ricky out of his seat and beat the bigot right out of him.

Sexual harassment? Was he serious? Had he looked in the mirror in the past 40 years? His skin was dry enough to sell as an alligator bag knock-off.

After I spoke with the pilots, I raced to the back galley to update Coco and Regal on the Rickocalypse. I never finished picking up trash; I just marched down the aisle with the bag flopping in my hand.

I addressed Coco, "Don't talk to him for the rest of the flight. Stay away from him. Don't even look at him unless we are evacuating the airplane, and if that happens, throw him the fuck out and make sure he misses the emergency slide."

Regal took my arm, "What happened? Are you okay?"

"He asked for a beer, and when I told him we weren't serving him any alcohol, he said, 'if either one of you talks to me again, I will report you for sexual harassment.' I got so angry that I called the pilots and told them to have security meet the airplane.

They stared at me in shock while I paced in the galley. Ricky's comment was more than an ignorant threat. It was a threat to our livelihoods. Can you imagine the bullshit we'd deal with having to explain a sexual harassment complaint from a passenger?

My mind was fogged with frustration that day in the galley, but when I think about it now, I realize any complaint from Ricky would have fallen on deaf ears. My airline has many gays working at our corporate office. One look at Ricky's scarred face, yellow stained fingernails, and wax-coated cotton balls stuck to the outside of his carry on bag, they'd have instantly known no rational thinking gay man would sexually harass a troll like him.

Justin James from the Houston Texans? Yes. If he boarded my flight, management better start the termination process the moment he takes his seat. Ricky, the homophobe who murdered his ostrich? Not so much.

Flight attendants deal with ridiculous bullshit on a daily basis. And before anyone stops me in the airport pointing their fake nails at me shouting, "That's your job, Joe!" I completely agree. Yes, our job is to deal with asshole airline passengers.

It's written somewhere in our hiring packet: *Your job, as a flight attendant, is to deal with asshole airline passengers.*

But the thought of having an ostrich-killing, Marlboro Red-smoking, homo-hating, country bumpkin threaten me with a sexual harassment complaint pushed me over my anger threshold. I am only human, something that airline passengers seem to forget each time I board a flight.

I ignored Ricky whenever I walked by row five hoping he'd choke on a piece of hard candy so I could say, "What? Huh? I'm sorry, I can't make out what you're saying through all your wheezing."

An hour before we landed, Regal made her way to the front of the airplane to start collecting trash. When she passed by Ricky, she told us his entire demeanor changed the moment he saw a female flight attendant.

My bad, stewardess.

Ricky believed that Regal was there to save him from us. He stopped her at the row and reiterated back about the beer, the sexual harassment threat, and that he didn't like dealing with guys like us.

She asked, "What do you mean, guys like them?"

"Gay guys. They ain't right."

She leaned against row four and let him have it, "You know, they're amazing guys. They're wonderful. You should be ashamed of how you're speaking about them. You just need to sit there until we land and not say anything else." With that, she walked away and continued collecting trash. At least she finished picking up trash; I have yet been able to manage how to do that when I am angry.

When the airplane landed and parked at the gate, Coco and I stood up to disarm our doors and we were surprised to see Ricky jump up out of his seat, grab his bag from the overhead bin, and push his way to the front of the aisle.

I rolled my eyes and whispered to Coco, "What happened to barely being able to walk?"

Ricky must have thought we were going to rape him once all the other passengers deplaned. An ass raping will make the slowest motherfucker move like a high school sprinter. I don't know for sure, but that might be the cure for immobility in senior citizens.

The airplane door opened and he briskly walked past us and disappeared down the jet bridge. Cousin Bobby, who barely said two words during the entire flight, came up right behind him and slowed down to apologize for his cousin's actions. I thanked him for the kind words and also thanked him for not shitting himself during the flight.

The last thing we needed was to deal with a shitty window seat while managing a homophobic old coot.

The moment the two of them stepped off the airplane, I followed behind pointing them out to the gate agent on the jet bridge. The Bloods & Crips would have thought I was attempting to start a gang war with the hand signs I was throwing around trying to point out Ricky to the gate agent. Once the gate agent knew what I was doing, he pulled Ricky aside to wait for the police. Immediately after the last passenger stepped off the airplane, I bolted like lightning halfway up the jet bridge to where our corporate security and the police were talking with him.

Once I finished briefing the police officer he asked me point blank, "Do you want to press charges? We'll arrest him right now."

Maybe I was the one who'd be on *Let's Make A Deal*. What other options did I have? What was behind door number two? A new car? A first-class seat on my commute home? I didn't know if pressing charges was what I wanted to do. I fantasized about him choking to death on a hard piece of candy, or maybe having a massive heart attack while talking to the police — but not going to jail.

I had a hard decision to make. "What happens if I press charges?"

The police officer pulled me aside,"If you press charges we'll take him to jail right now. You'll have to show up for a court date."

He lost me at a court date. I had no desire to see Ricky ever again. He used up enough of my energy to run a half marathon. Was it enough having the police scare the shit out of him? Was it my job to teach him a lesson? Would that even matter? Was my ego hurt to the point that I couldn't see through my anger? All these questions flooded my mind while standing next to Coco and Regal. On the airplane, I had so much fury that I was willing to miss my commute home to make sure he paid for his threat.

But now, I didn't know what to do. It became clear that I had let my ego run wild. I had taken Ricky's words personally instead of being the bigger person and allowing what he said to roll off my back. Most of us are prone to do that, but I should know better than to let someone like him have that much control over my emotions. As a gay man, I've spent decades listening to uneducated strangers sling homophobic slurs at me. Hell, even my mother did it.

Sure, Ricky needed to believe he might never step foot on an airplane again for being an ignorant asshole, but my job wasn't to destroy his life. As I looked over at him, barely able to stand against the wall of the jet bridge, I realized he was a mess. The only happiness he probably ever experienced was that ostrich, and we all know how that turned out. My chapter in Ricky's saga had come to a close.

250

"No. I don't want to press charges. Just make sure Ricky knows he can't talk to flight attendants like that."

The police officer shook my hand and walked over to the crowd surrounding Ricky.

Coco, Regal, and I headed down the jet bridge towards the gate area when Bobby stopped me again to apologize. I nodded with a civil smile, "Thank you. I have nothing else to say; I have a flight to catch." I continued walking towards the door and never turned back.

The next time I hear the words wheelchair, diarrhea, or ostrich on my flight — I think I'll call in sick.

Journal Entry:
Reserve (Not For Me)... Again

Dear Journal,

Did my first kettlebell workout this morning and it was electric. My entire body exploded like ISIS was all up inside me. I don't have to worry about ISIS inside me — I'm not a goat. It's true. Did you know they were goat fuckers? Neither did I until I looked it up online. Goat fuckers. I mean, not even a horse... but a goat. I guess the back kick isn't as bad from a goat as a horse. I wouldn't know, I am not into bestiality.

I don't even like jerking off when my cats are in the room.

My morning was pretty uneventful. I paid a few bills online, had some breakfast, and chatted with Justin on the phone. Bidding for my August schedule closed three days ago, and they still haven't released our schedules.

Around 12:15 p.m. I checked online and I noticed the August schedules posted. I clicked on the tab for August, and a warm feeling instantly rushed through me. My biggest fear had become a reality. You'd think my biggest concern was crashing into the ocean and having my legs torn off by force, but that's not the case. That's nothing compared to going back on fucking reserve. When I saw the reserve days lined up on my schedule like angry little soldiers, I almost did a Linda Blair impression on my laptop. I am not exaggerating. As I write this, I have the urge to projectile vomit all over the apartment, including the cats. The inside of my stomach was hanging onto my tonsils ready to create breakfast art on the walls. It's the feeling of devastation that comes with the death of a loved one. I was more upset over this than when my mother died. When she died, I was sad, but it was over rather quickly.

Being on reserve would last me an entire month.

It was all too shocking. I had to down some gout medication because the intense level of stress began triggering an attack. The apartment could have burned down to the pavement, with me inside it, and I'd have been thrilled I avoided going back on reserve. I keep clicking refresh on the computer hoping change would come. There would be no change. This wasn't Obama becoming president; this was the effects of being based at LAX.

Was all this that serious? Yes, it was fucking devastating. This was more upsetting than the time I accidentally ran over a feral kitten in my driveway. Wait, I take that back — that was life-changing. I continue having nightmares about that kitty pancake. My two cats still curl their lips up at me in disgust, and one of them wasn't even born during my kitty murder phase.

But it's been years since I was on reserve. Years! I have no clue how to be on reserve. And let's face it, when I was on reserve the first time around, I was a fucking disaster. Within five minutes of clicking on my August schedule, I created an entire story in my irrational mind that bad things were on the horizon for me, which included my termination.

I also assumed it was kitty pancake coming back for his/her revenge.

After staring at my laptop for a few hours — I can't believe I didn't throw it across the room — I finally stood up from my chair, moved to the kitchen, paced for a few minutes, and then returned to the desk. I'd let out one of my loud, crazy laughs and then fight back the tears. I hadn't cried yet, but I wanted to. I wanted to cry harder than that time I sat in my car after watching *Titanic* for the first time. If I was having a nervous breakdown — or better yet, a heart attack — I hoped I died sooner than later. I also wished Matt got home before the cats started snacking on my fingertips.

I texted Matt, but he was unavailable. That's what happens when you have a successful husband, he's married to his job and is unavailable to take your call while you contemplate feeding yourself to the cats.

It's probably for the best because I was unhinged. I blamed everyone for me going back on reserve in LAX. Everyone! I blamed senior flight attendants for transferring in. I blamed junior flight attendants for transferring out. I blamed management for treating LAX like that drunk uncle that never gets invited to Thanksgiving because he's on the sex offenders registry. I blamed myself, but not that much. I criticized my husband for moving us to California where I had to deal with a shitty work schedule while he worked three miles away. I even blamed my cat Tucker when he meowed for more cat treats. Who's fucking thinking about cat treats at a time like this?

By this time I could barely make it to the bathroom without crying. I went through two boxes of tissues and hadn't even jerked off. This was a catastrophe. I needed Anderson Cooper outside my apartment door giving a play-by-play of my psychotic break. All I thought about was downing three bottles of wine and sleeping until September 1.

I complained to anyone who answered my text messages. Trick Daddy told me to have a backup plan. He was right. He's usually right.

If he knew I said that, he'd never let me hear the end of it.

Instead of drinking all that wine, even though it sounded smart at the time, I started playing out different scenarios in my head. I could drive my car down to LA, but I had no place to sleep. I figured I could sleep in my car. That's depressing. I'm married, make decent money, have a job, and I'd be homeless in LA. Let that sink in for a moment. People working in the fast food industry have it better than I do.

I'd join the local 24 Hour Fitness to use their showers. Then I'd hang out at Starbucks as much as possible and sleep in the flight attendant lounge. Let's hope management doesn't kick me out, even though this was entirely their fault. Justin offered to let me stay with him in San Diego. That was kind. And there was always the dirty roach infested motel option if I was in dire need of accommodations.

Maybe this wasn't the end of the world. I'd be a senior reserve flight attendant for the month, so I'd have the opportunity to pick up trips on my reserve days. Another positive note, I was awarded all the days off I needed for my vacation. Think positive, Joe. I already felt better. I laughed again and told myself, "Fuck it. Things always work out."

Matt walked in the house while I sat at the desk tapping away on my laptop. I swung the chair to face him, "I'm back on reserve next month. I've had a terrible day."

He placed his laptop bag on the table and responded, "Me too. I was so busy at work I couldn't attend my yoga class after lunch."

I knew he meant well, but my first instinct — and I am not ashamed to admit this — was to punch him square in the balls. Maybe even cut the fuckers off. I refused to respond because I was stunned by what I took as an inconsiderate response.

I try not to blame him for moving us to California where I have spent most of my time dealing with terrible schedules or commuting cross country. But to compare going back on reserve to missing a yoga class? Am I crazy thinking there is something wrong with that sentence? Why doesn't he slap me on my head and kick me in the face? I pushed my feelings down. I refused to show my anger, but I am sure my neck and face were red as if I laid out in the sun all day without sunscreen.

We moved the conversation to the living room. I sat across from Matt and tried speaking in a calm and relaxed manner; that lasted about three seconds. I fell apart and erupted my entire day onto him. An emotional bukkake raged on throughout the apartment while he sat there listening to me like a well-paid therapist. Repeating myself incoherently, my voice shifted from a tween to a three pack a day smoker. He watched me without saying a word. At least he's smart. Without realizing it, my hands waved through the air while I retold my dilemma. I don't know why I do this, but something tells me it helps me speak faster when I'm an emotional wreck.

When I eventually dumped all the drama out, these were the following concerns addressed:

I am on reserve after seven and a half years

I need to drive the car down to Los Angeles

I have no crashpad

There are no crashpads

I have no place to sleep

I want to die

I will be fired by August 2

When I had nothing else to say and stopped to take a break, Matt spoke in a soothing voice, "Are you done?" I stared at him, "I guess you are." His resolution was quick, "We'll find you a month rental for August that's within your reserve call out time. Drive the car down, and I'll just bike and take the bus to work. You'll be fine. Remember, nothing bad has happened yet."

With that feedback, I felt instantly relieved, as if he handed me a handful of Chill The Fuck Out tablets and a bottle of whiskey.

He added, "We may not break even for August, but we'll be fine."

Instantly, being back on reserve wasn't the disaster I had imagined. Don't get me wrong, it sucked tremendously, but after talking with Matt, it almost sounded manageable.

We headed to the train station to catch a baseball game in San Francisco. Matt's company has a suite, and we'd gone a few times. It's nice. I figured that was the perfect way to take my mind off what I had put myself through all day. Or should I say, what the airline put me through all day?

While we stood at the train station, I received an email from my LAX base manager. In my psychotic state — and let's not sugar coat it, I was a crazy bitch — I had forgotten entirely about emailing him. When I initially saw my August schedule, I threw myself at his mercy asking about taking a leave of absence.

That had been four hours earlier. My manager finally responded and informed me that there were available spots to apply for leave, but if I wanted one, I had to call and put in my request as soon as possible because they were on a first come, first serve basis.

I called the number he gave me while trains zipped down the tracks. By the time our train pulled up, I had submitted my request. By the time we arrive in San Francisco, he had approved it. By the time we were in the company suite, and I had downed a few beers, my supervisor called to confirm my leave of absence. It was that easy.

The Universe looked out for me in a big way. Sure, it would have been nice if it had looked out for me much sooner, before the crazy hand-talking and emotional bukkake, but I'll take good news from the Universe whenever offered to me.

The Job Reference

Tears for Fears sang the song, "Everybody Wants To Rule The World" but I believe that everybody wants a flight attendant job reference. If you are a flight attendant, you know what I am talking about. If you are not a flight attendant but you know one, you also know what I am talking about. I've been asked to provide a job reference on more than one occasion. Obtaining a referral for an airline job is a life-changing opportunity. A Scientologist would probably reconcile with an excommunicated sibling for an airline job reference.

I imagine the phone call would go something like, "Hi Debbie. Listen, I know we haven't talked in a few years because you gave up on Scientology after watching *Leah Remini: Scientology and the Aftermath*, but let's say we just forget about all that Xenu nonsense and you get me an interview at your airline."

That's how intense applicants get about airline job references. They'd give up their belief in L. Ron. Hubbard to snag a seat at an interview. The minute a family member, friend you severed ties with, or disgruntled neighbor knows you work for the airlines; you will ultimately — at some point — become bombarded with, "When are the airlines hiring? I'm thinking about becoming a flight attendant."

It takes more than a casual, "I'm thinking about…" when it comes to putting my neck on the chopping block to give someone a job reference. I'm sorry, but that's how it goes. You don't just hand out these golden tickets like Halloween candy. This isn't *Willy Wonka and the Chocolate Factory*; this is the airline industry. I'm more stingy writing letters of recommendation than I am handing out buddy passes. My concern, and what should be everyone's concern when giving a reference is, what if the person turns out to be a total fuck up? It's a fact — I know this from experience — that the millisecond the person you spoke highly of begins receiving more complaint letters at work than Hollywood producers receive sexual harassment claims, your boss will be all over you quicker than Kevin Spacey boning up at an all-boys high school musical.

And I do an excellent job at making myself look terrible enough at my airline.

A few years back, someone put me in an awkward position that would ultimately test me as a human being. My ex-boyfriend Kurt's ex-boyfriend Doug (I hope that didn't confuse you because it confused the hell out of me for a brief second) sent me a random text message. I had no clue who it was or how he got my number, but I'd later learn that Kurt gave it to him.

Doug's text read: *Hi Joe. Do you have a minute to answer some questions about becoming a flight attendant? I hear your airline is hiring.*

Who is this?

He replied a few minutes later: *It's Doug Humerekr.*

At first, I didn't think anything of it. Why would I care about a text message from Doug? We had a dramatic history together, but through the years we learned how to be civil towards each other in public. There were no hard feelings, or so I thought. Anyway, Kurt and I had separated over a decade ago, and the two of them had recently ended their decade-long relationship. Time had healed all past wounds and left so much water under the bridge; I'd need a horse to wade across to the other side.

During the text conversation, Doug rattled off random questions about life as a flight attendant, inquiries that rarely have one easy answer, such as: Can I be based at home? Where will I be based? How much will I make? How many flights will I work in a day?… and so on. I was happy to answer them to the best of my ability. Why not, right? All he was doing was interviewing me like Barbara Walters, and we all know I love a good interview.

And then these words popped up on my cell phone: *Would you give me a reference?*

Tic Toc. Tic Toc. If I were a 30-something single woman with five cats, you would have thought it was my biological clock ticking, But no, it was just the seconds that crept by while I pondered how to answer. Did I go the dick move and laugh at him? Did I forgive and forget and write him the reference? It seemed like an obvious answer; I'd do what was unexpected of me. I'd be the good guy. No, I'd be the great guy. I made my decision and responded: *Sure. Let's talk on the phone in a few days. I can answer more of your questions.*

Unbeknownst to me, my emotions would attack me velociraptor-style when I least expected it.

To be honest, I felt proud that I was willing to offer him a reference. Initially, I had no issues referring him to my airline. But as the seconds turned into passing minutes, and those minutes turned into many hours, by the end of the night, it hit me straight in the face: What the fuck was I thinking? Had I been the victim of an alien abduction? Was I living in a real life *Invasion of the Body Snatchers*? Did I fall and damage my medial temporal lobe resulting in amnesia?

Seriously, had I forgotten that this asshole stole my boyfriend right out from under my nose? Well, that's not exactly the truth. He stole Kurt right out from under me during our vacation to Atlanta.

But to understand this completely, I'll have to take you back to Orlando, Florida on December 5, 1999. On that crisp December evening, my friend Gary and I decided to head out for a few drinks to the local bear bar, The Full Moon Saloon. The Full Moon Saloon was a dark, smoke-fill den of restroom stall blowjobs, drugs, underage drinking, and country music that made me feel right at home, like being back in my mother's womb. And because my mother smoked like a brush fire while she was pregnant with me, I'm not exaggerating when I say it felt like being back in her cozy smoke-stained uterus.

After a few hours, a handful of beers, and the occasional button undone on my shirt; I set my sights on a tall, attractive looking gentleman standing against the wall holding a beer in his hand. I went in for the kill — we are bears after all — and after a dull conversation regarding *Star Wars: The Phantom Menace*, we scheduled a date at Downtown Disney.

A week later, we met up at the Virgin Megastore, where Kurt's eyebrows raised the moment he saw Gary tagging alone.

We hugged, and he tried being funny, "Do you always bring your friend on a date with you?"

Before I could answer, Gary stepped in, "Yes he does. Consider me here on behalf of his mother."

We laughed, but I instantly wanted to slap myself — and Gary — for inviting him along on my date. After my mother, Gary was the next big cockblock in my life.

I shrugged my shoulders, laughed off Gary's outrageous comment, and spent the night dancing and making out with Kurt on the dance floor at 8Trax, a 70's/80's club. A few weeks, and a couple of dates later, I moved into his corner end townhouse. It happened so fast I had to check to make sure we weren't lesbians. No U-haul rented, so we were good to go.

Kurt drove a white Toyota Camry, was the dad to a small annoying dog and had graduated from nursing school the previous summer. He was a dreamboat, and he was all mine. Santa Claus came quickly that year, and now that I finally had a full-time boyfriend, so did I.

Our relationship was a whirlwind romance. We loved each other one month, hated each other the next. In a year, we broke up, got back together, and fell madly in love with each other all over again. I am not proud of this, but I was extremely psychotic regarding my passion for him.

For example, the first time we separated, during autumn of 2000, my cat Lucy and I relocated to our own one bedroom apartment. Did we move to another town? Did we move across town? Hell, did we move five miles away?

No!

We moved to an apartment complex precisely two miles away. Who does that? A lunatic, that's who. Don't worry though; I never pined for him outside his kitchen window while devouring a box of Oreo cookies crying to "Pinch Me" by the Barenaked Ladies. My pining and tears were saved for when I was home alone, sitting on my Rooms To Go sofa, and blaming Lucy for scratching up the screened-in patio one too many times.

Was that enough of my crazy obsessed love?

No!

Not only did I move two miles away, but I also doubled down on my crazy by transferring to the same hospital Kurt worked at so the chance of us bumping into each would multiply... and it did. We saw each other daily, even though we worked on separate units. I'd often find myself "lost" on the telemetry floor where he worked meandering around as if I belonged.

One afternoon in September, he strolled up to me at the nurse's station and handed me a plastic-wrapped copy of Madonna's *Music* CD. "I thought you might enjoy this."

I held the gift in my hand and fought back the urge to sit on his face. For one, I was standing at the nurse's station, probably not the place to jump on someone's face. And two, I didn't want to smother him after he had brought me such a thoughtful gift. I knew we'd be back together and I was correct. Within a week, Lucy and I moved back into the townhouse with our heart's filled with love and my credit report filled with a broken apartment lease.

One of the stupidest decisions of my life.

The status quo was amicable for about six months. We'd argue but quickly reconcile. Kurt held my hand in the living room when I'd cry about my relationship with my mother, and then I'd return the favor after we'd visit his mother and she'd say nasty things to me like, "The dog probably thinks you're fat."

Like I said, status quo until one night when we went out for drinks and met new friends at The Full Moon Saloon. One new friend, Doug, and an acquaintance I knew from high school, Jason.

When we met them, Doug and Jason had been dating for a few years. They owned a home together on Florida's east coast and honestly seemed happier than Kurt and I. I was envious of them. While Kurt and I fought over what time to leave the bar, Doug and Jason agreed unanimously. When we started hanging out with them, it was a relief to meet a gay couple who were monogamous and looking for new friends. We spent a few weekends hanging out together — them at the townhouse, us at their house — and Doug and I connected with our love for Madonna. Admiration for Madonna that usually binds queens together forever. It was such a bond that Kurt and Jason would mock us while we sat in Doug's living room deliberating which Madonna single we felt was the best song ever. Which video was her best video ever? What album was her best? And so on.

One night, Kurt looked over at us from the sofa while we sat on the floor looking through Madonna CDs and said, "*Music*? A CD called music? What's she going to do next? Write a book and call it book?"

Not funny at the time, but hilarious now.

Jason and I eventually connected after spending an entire evening chasing a guy around the bar who attended our high school. Not just an average guy, a guy we never — in a billion fucking years — expected to see at a gay bar. A hot ex-high school football player named, Hank Marsh, who we followed around the bar like two hungry teenage girls who bumped into a drunk Joey Fatone at a dance club. Pathetic, but fun as hell.

About a month later — give or take a week — Kurt, Doug, Jason, and I decided to take a long weekend trip to Georgia. The day before we were scheduled to leave, Doug called the house in distress, "Hey Joe. Can you talk?"

"Yeah. What's up?" I asked putting away the dishes.

"Jason just told me that he doesn't want to go on vacation. I don't know what to do. I still want to go," his voice was shaking and upset, "is it okay if only the three of us go?"

"Yeah. Of course," I didn't think to ask Kurt, "just drive over tonight, and we can leave early in the morning."

"Is that going to be okay with Kurt?"

"You know what, he just walked in from outside. Let me ask him, and I'll call you back."

When Kurt came in from walking the dogs — by this time we had two — I briefed him on the situation, and he was more than eager for us to continue our vacation plans sans Jason. In fact, he promptly called Doug and suggested he hightail his ass over to the townhouse, and we'd depart that evening. A few hours later, with the dog sitter rescheduled to start a day earlier, the three of us were on our way to Atlanta with a quick overnight in Macon.

During the car ride along Interstate 75, Doug informed us that things between him and Jason had gone south since we'd seen them last. Jason became distant and tended to avoid him when they were at home. Kurt comforted Doug and advised him as a brother might to his younger sibling. From the back seat, I watched as Kurt carefully chose his words to ease Doug's distress and I loved him even more for being so caring and thoughtful to another human being.

After dinner in Macon, we went back to the hotel, and the mood promptly shifted. Kurt caught me off guard when he casually suggested the three of us masturbate together.

The idea was intriguing, but my instincts held me back. In the end, I was too weak to turn down Kurt's suggestion.

I think this might be the perfect point to say: NEVER HAVE A THREESOME WITH YOUR BOYFRIEND AND A FRIEND!

A few weeks later, Kurt and Doug were a couple. And my heart sat in a clear glass bowl in front of the meat grinder.

All those feelings fired back at me while faced with the dilemma of providing Doug with a job reference. Not just any job reference, but *THE* job reference. Like I said before, the life-changing job reference. How many pillows, blankets, and bottles of wine would he swipe off the airplane? If he could steal my boyfriend from me, he would inevitably pilfer enough off the plane to impact my profit sharing.

And then I had a thought, after our entire history, and the betrayal he put me through all those years ago, he dared ask me to do something kind. Not even nice — nice would be not slapping him silly with a beer bottle — but to help him get a job at my airline and change his life for the better. Did he live in an alternate universe where stabbing a friend in the back rewards you with a job referral?

How dare he ask me for anything. A sip of water in the desert, yes, but a fucking job?

I had a lot to digest, and my mind buzzed like a beehive. Yes, Doug made a mistake in 2001. He came into my home, befriended my boyfriend and me, and aided in destroying my relationship with Kurt. There's no denying my emotional escapades had a part to play in the demise of our partnership, but who blames themselves in a time of loss? I had to ask myself, am I innocent of making terrible mistakes of my own?

On the flip side, if Doug hadn't wedged himself between us, it would have just been another person. Kurt and I were destined to end in a pile of rubble. We were never meant to last. In all honesty, I should have thanked Doug. I should have walked right up into the flight attendant interview and begged them to hire him. Fire me if you have to, just hire him. I owed him my freedom from Kurt, freedom that gave me the chance to venture out and find the real love I was meant to have. Doug deserved gratitude for saving me from years of disappointment in a relationship doomed from the beginning.

I'm serious, a boyfriend who peels shrimp for you on your second date will never last. Take my word for it; I know first hand.

And let's not forget, Doug wasn't the only guilty person in this reality television drama. Kurt and I were just as guilty. The only ones not guilty were the two dogs and my cat, Lucy.

When I felt confident about my feelings for Doug, I decided to give him the job reference. I took a deep relaxing breath, and without warning, my brain bitch slapped me.

Smack! What the fuck are you thinking, Joe Thomas?

And agreed, what the fuck was I thinking? The level of confusion floating throughout my head was astounding. How could I justify helping a man who pretended to be my friend while stabbing me in the back with a dull knife listening to Madonna's *Erotica* CD? It seemed like a running theme in my life; meet Joe, befriend him, and when he turns around to change out the CD, stab him in the back. It took years to forgive Doug, but never would I be able to forget what he had done. For me that meant, I held no personal ill feelings towards him — or wished him harm — and I hoped he had a great life, but I did not want him coming around asking for help. Except, as I hinted before, if we were lost in the desert together and I had a bottle of water.

I may be indifferent towards you, but I won't let you die.

Another question popped up, did I feel comfortable working with him on an airplane? Let me ask, would anyone feel comfortable working in a metal tube, at 38,000 feet, with someone they didn't trust? And I don't mean just because they lied to you about why they were late for report time. I mean, because they were untrustworthy and proved it to you personally. Could I give him, who I wouldn't trust with my cell phone charger, an opportunity of a lifetime? It's a difficult question that kept me awake for a few nights. One that left me perplexed throughout the entire ordeal.

Then I thought about revenge. Who doesn't love exacting revenge on someone who has done them wrong?

In my defense, I'm a Scorpio, and if you believe in astrology — I only do when it suits my need for revenge — you know that Scorpios don't get mad, they get even. Seeking revenge for my shattered heart perked me up and sat on the tip of my tongue like a dab of Sriracha. I laid in bed practically tasting it. Scenario after scenario crowded my already confused brain. My favorite was to interview him myself (I was trained to conduct interviews at the airline), lead him to believe he surpassed every other applicant, and then send him a denial email covered in smiley emojis three months later. I had a few friends in human resources; I'd pull a few strings and make it happen.

The next day I talked to Matt about it. "What do you think I should do?"

He splashed around in the hot tub, "Well, why do you care? If he gets the job, then he gets the job. You're only giving him a reference."

"Why do I have to be the better person?"

"Because you are. And you want to be, right?"

"Yes. I guess I can give Doug the reference and if he gets the job, then he deserves it."

Input from different people made things even more confusing. When I texted Trick Daddy for his guidance, he flatly responded: *Fuck that! Don't be trying to get someone like that a job with us. He's a terrible person. He stole your boyfriend. He's obviously trash.*

I sincerely agreed with him, but my heart swayed me in a different direction. While my brain told me to hang him upside down in front of the departure level at Orlando International Airport for every passenger leaving Disney to see, my heart told me to be the better person. I've learned that being the better person is never easy when conflicted with emotions, but it's undeniably the way we should strive to be.

When Doug and I spoke on the phone a few days later, I was extremely friendly. I pushed whatever animosity I had all the way down to the tips of my toes, "When you go to the interview, I want you to ask for Manny Cruz. He's gonna be in Orlando that day conducting interviews." I continued, "Just go up to him and say, 'Hi. I'm Doug Humerekr. Joe Thomas told me to come over and say hi.'"

"Sounds good." he replied, "I'm gonna send you a picture of me in a brown and a blue suit. Let me know which one looks better." We hung up the call, and a few minutes later my cell phone alerted me with his text message.

I responded: *Wear the blue suit. Make sure you wear a red tie. The interviewers will love that.*

He countered: *I don't know about the suit. My friend works there and said I should go with the brown suit.*

I was offended. I'm trained to conducted interviews and know what they're looking for during the interview process. And to be completely honest, Doug looked better in the blue suit: *Who's your friend? How long has he been here?*

He's still in training.

I got nasty: *I don't want to sound like a dick, but he's been here for five seconds. I've been here for eight years. I'd listen to me.*

That's all the help I gave him, and let's face it, in the world of airline industry interviews if you don't get the job after all that insider help, including a contact person AT the interview, you don't deserve it.

Apparently, he didn't deserve it.

A few days after his interview, I waited for him to text. A call or text might have been polite after giving him the reference, but apparently — and it should come as no surprise — he was not polite. Finally, I texted him: *Hey, how did it go?*

I believe he responded a few hours later: *I got confirmation today. I didn't get it.*

I was slightly surprised but expected it. How did Doug fuck it up? I practically handed him the pamphlet on how to get hired. I dug deep into questions: *Did you wear a red tie?*

Yes. He responded.

I pushed for more information: *Did you smile? Did you work as a team during the group session?*

Yes. I did all that. I wore the blue suit. I should have worn another one.

I replied: *That doesn't matter. You wore a suit. Some bitches wear sweaters three sizes too large. I'm sure it wasn't the suit. Did you introduce yourself to Manny?*

No. I didn't feel comfortable.

There it was. I instructed Doug to introduce himself to my friend, Manny, and he didn't do it. Manny and I had known each other for years. Even though Manny would not have given Doug particular treatment, it helps to have a mutual connection with an interviewer.

Who the fuck asks for a reference and your assistance, and when you give it, they don't follow your advice?

I felt pleasure now: *That was it. You should have let Manny know who you were.*

He was persistent: *No, Joe. It was the suit. I can apply in 6 months. I'll wear a different outfit next time.*

I left the conversation alone after that but thought to myself; I hope you wear it for an interview at a different airline.

We All Need Balcony People Part III

(Seriously, how many parts are there to this story?)

Did you think the Evan story was over? Not exactly.

On New Year's Eve, I received a text message from an unknown number; it was Evan. We had not spoken in over four months, and I was surprised to hear from him. In typical Evan humor, he started the conversation by texting: *Knock Knock.*

Then he followed it up with a 9/11 joke while wishing Matt and me a happy New Year.

Our conversation was light and brief. I appreciated Evan reaching out to me, but it sent up a red flag in my brain. Did I want to go down this road again? On the one hand, I was ecstatic my friend, who I had spent countless hours traveling and laughing with, was contacting me. On the other hand, I remembered that we could not fix our fractured friendship with a band-aid.

Was his text message a band-aid? Was it time to mend our friendship?

Was that even possible? More questions than answers flooded my brain. I had no clue what to think, so I did something a little different, I put down the red flag and stopped dwelling on what the future might bring. For that brief moment, I merely enjoyed our connection.

I've learned one thing from this experience. When you've had a falling out with a close friend, you owe it to yourselves — and the friendship — to try and make amends.

THE END

Acknowledgements

The first person I would like to thank is ME! It's hard to write a book; I need all that acknowledgment I can get.

None of this would be possible if not for my husband, Matthew. You've lifted me up when I was down, and you have encouraged me through the good times, the bad times, and all the in-between times. I love you.

To Michael Sistrunk, you are the brother I never had. You have always been there to lend an ear, and I am grateful. I'd also like to take this opportunity to apologize publicly for spilling alcohol on your sofa and acting like a stripper during your holiday party in 2017. I hope this apology makes up for it.

To Adam Richardson, I couldn't have asked for a more incredible friend in the entire ~~galaxy~~ UNIVERSE! You are too special for words (well, except for those words that I just typed out). Thank you for your honesty and advice regarding the book cover, I needed that.

To Russ Brucker and Sharon Brucker, you've made an only child with no living parents feel loved. What a wonderful gift!

To Sarah Brucker, thank you for being the best sister-in-law I have ever had. Yes, you are the only one I have ever had, but that's not important. The important thing is, you are the BEST.

To the incredibly talented, Ryan Lopez, you brought my book to life AGAIN, and I can't thank you enough. I've even forgiven you for hinting that my head was an odd shape and difficult to draw.

To Laura Jean Salerno, my writing wife. What can I say? You've been enriching my life since the day we met. Thank you for taking the time out of your hectic life to write the foreword for my book. And just so it's on record, I did not pay you to write those lovely things. Thank you.

To my mother, Irene, thank you for trying your best. That's all we can do in life.

Now for the rest in alphabetical order. I'd like to clarify, not everyone I am directly acknowledging assisted in the creation of this book. What these individuals have done is something even more significant, more powerful. They have brought me joy. They have challenged me to think big. Some are still here with us, and some have passed on. They have pushed me to my limits and stood with me at the finishing line. They have all positively influenced me to be a better person.

For that, I thank you all from my bottom of my heart. I am sure I will miss some people, but please don't email me, text me, or call me because I left out your name. It's hard remembering everyone who has touched me in my life.

Adam Willis, Alanna Reynolds, Alex Batista, Arleen Begen, Barbara Brown, Brandon Arrington, Cynthia Libby Fillion, David Roberts, David Chimento, Deirdre Harris, Eric Rodriguez, Garon Wade, Gloria Saur, Heather Poole, Jake Saur, Jason "Chops" Grodzinsky, Jenn Punky Tessem, John Ford, John Kieffner, John Stripling, Joseph Adams,

Joshua Cook, Kelly W. Woodland, Ken Foskey, Mary Ann Jameson, Matthew DeBonee, Matthew Riviera, Mark Smith, Melissa Villanueva, Michael Johns, Michael Wagner, Renee Kueser, Robert Amerison, Robert Huss, Roberta Marowitz, Ryan Hawkins, Ryan Spellman, Sara Willis, Sarah Ford, Sarah Kieffner, Shannon Forrest, Shawn Murray, Terry Kisler, Thomas Kelly, Tim Poweleny, Todd Lewis, Tom Koser, Tyson Jackson, and William "Bill" Filaretos.

And last, but not certainly least, thank you to all the amazing flight attendants, pilots, gate agents, mechanics, ground operations, supervisors, managers, and everyone else who has made me laugh, allowed me to harass them sexually, and given me a reason to write about them in this book.

Who Let This Guy Author A Book?

Joe Thomas is a writer, blogger, flight attendant, homosexual, and lover of wine. He currently lives in the San Francisco Bay Area with his husband, Matt, and their two cats, Tucker and Harvey.

71697800R00174

Made in the USA
Columbia, SC
26 August 2019